th Demise of Big Bands;
Become Furniture Store

JOSEPH BARRY KILLED
BY TRAIN IN FAIRFIELD
Post 7 May 1962

27 Injured at Ritz Dance
As Promenade Collapses
Post 17 Sept. 1945

-RITZ BALLROOM;
OF 'BIG BANDS'

It's Joe Barry Night
Sun. Post 10, Dec. 1961
Wednesday at Ritz

Ray Colonari, Band Fan As a Boy,
Named Assistant Manager of Ritz
Post 31 Oct 1948

Home of Happy Dancers

The Story of Bridgeport, Connecticut's
RITZ BALLROOM

THE
DONNING COMPANY
PUBLISHERS

At the Ritz

At the Ritz . . . where nights are all aglow

At the Ritz . . . where music's sweet and low

In each other's arms . . . let's cuddle tight

And then share the charms of one sweet night.

At the Ritz . . . where "Dreams Come True" are abound

At the Ritz . . . where all "Love Lost" is found

For a new romance . . . this is our chance

At the Ritz . . . let's sing and dance.

Like so many dance lovers,
the unknown fan who wrote this
dedication to the ballroom owners
on the occasion of their Silver Jubilee
shared many a "sweet night."

The above is from
"ALMOST EVERYONE PUT ON THE RITZ"
by Deborah Rick
Bridgeport Post—February 7, 1983

Home of Happy Dancers

THE HAPPINESS BOYS
George S. McCormack & Joseph R. Barry

The Story of Bridgeport, Connecticut's
RITZ BALLROOM

by Jeffrey C. Williams

Copyright © 2011 by Jeffrey C. Williams
Second printing 2012

All rights reserved, including the right to reproduce this work in any form whatsoever without permission in writing from the publisher, except for brief passages in connection with a review. For information, please write:

The Donning Company Publishers
184 Business Park Drive, Suite 206
Virginia Beach, VA 23462

Steve Mull, General Manager
Barbara B. Buchanan, Office Manager
Richard A. Horwege, Senior Editor
Pamela Engelhard, Graphic Designer
Priscilla Odango, Imaging Artist
Susan Adams, Project Research Coordinator
Tonya Washam, Marketing Specialist
Pamela Engelhard, Marketing Advisor

Mary Miller, Project Director

Library of Congress Cataloging-in-Publication Data

Williams, Jeffrey C.
    Home of happy dancers : the story of Bridgeport, Connecticut's Ritz Ballroom / by Jeffrey C. Williams.
       p. cm.
    ISBN 978-1-57864-722-4 (hard cover : alk. paper)
1. Ritz Ballroom (Bridgeport, Conn.)—History. 2. Ballrooms—Connecticut—Bridgeport—History. 3. Ballroom dancing—Connecticut—Bridgeport—History. 4. Bridgeport (Conn.)—Social life and customs. I. Title.
    GV1750.4.W55 2011
    793.3'3097469—dc23

2011042442

Printed in the USA at Walsworth Publishing Company

*This Book is
Lovingly Dedicated to My Parents*

**Rosemary (Mercurio)
& Howard Williams**

Two of Those Happy Dancers!

Table of Contents

	FOREWORD by Les Brown, Jr.	8
	PROLOGUE	10
1	**THE EARLY YEARS**	14
2	***ALMOST EVERYONE 'PUT ON THE RITZ'** by Deborah Rick *Bridgeport Post*—February 7, 1983	18
3	***27 INJURED AT RITZ DANCE AS PROMENADE COLLAPSES** *Bridgeport Post*—September 17, 1945	22
4	***RAY COLONARI, BAND FAN AS BOY, NAMED ASSISTANT MANAGER OF RITZ** by Rocky Clark *Bridgeport Post*—October 31, 1948	26
5	***RAY COLONARI** *Union News*—Circa 1950	28
6	***JOEY ZELLE** *Union News*—September 1950	32
7	***OLD TIMES** with Joe Hurley *Bridgeport Herald*—June 14, 1952	36
8	***RITZ CANCELS ROCK 'N' ROLL BAND** *Bridgeport Sunday Post*—May 22, 1955	38
9	***RITZ MANAGER RECALLS HIS CAREER AS A NEWSPAPER BOY 50 YEARS AGO** *Bridgeport Post*—October 8, 1955	40
10	***SNAP SHOTS AND SHORT STORIES** by Edward W. Plaisted *Bridgeport Post*—February 3, 1958	42
11	***FAMED RITZ BALLROOM LEASED; WILL BECOME FURNITURE STORE** by Harry Neigher *Bridgeport Sunday Herald*—October 22, 1961	44
	COLORFUL MEMORIES	49
12	***RITZ PASSES WITH DEMISE OF BIG BANDS; BALLROOM LEASED TO BECOME FURNITURE STORE** by Roldo Bartimole *Bridgeport Sunday Post*—October 22, 1961	62
13	***IT'S JOE BARRY NIGHT WEDNESDAY AT THE RITZ** by Tom Magner *Bridgeport Sunday Post*—December 10, 1961	68
14	***JOSEPH BARRY KILLED BY TRAIN IN FAIRFIELD** *Bridgeport Herald*—May 7, 1962	70

15	*MUSIC ENDS FOR JOE BARRY AT WHISTLE STOP *Bridgeport Sunday Herald*—May 13, 1962	74
16	*FIRE RAZES EX-RITZ BALLROOM; ONE-TIME SITE OF 'BIG BANDS' by Frank DeCerbo *Bridgeport Post*—June 12, 1970	78
17	*RITZ HAD COLORFUL HISTORY WITH PROMS, BANDS, DINNERS *Bridgeport Post*—May 5, 1973	82
18	*RUDY VALLEE ONCE CROONED IN BRIDGEPORT by Mary K. Witkowski *Bridgeport News*—November 1, 2001	84
19	**THE RITZ** by Gene Hull From His Book *Hooked on a Horn*	86
20	**MEMORIES ARE MADE OF THIS**	92
	EPILOGUE	100
	ABOUT THE AUTHOR	101
	RESOURCES and ACKNOWLEDGMENTS	102
	HAPPY MEMORIES	103

*While researching I was often taken back in time by reading numerous press clippings and newspaper articles, some quite quaintly written. Each represented a major event in the Ritz's history, and each transported me to the exact time the event occurred. Rather than dilute these pieces of history with my own words, I have opted to showcase them, word for word, in chronological order so readers can experience the same feeling I had of "being there" when these events were actually happening. When available, the names of the writers of these pieces are indicated to credit them for their work.

I am sure many readers will remember, first-hand, these happenings. For others, and especially younger readers, I hope this "time warp" gives them a feeling of being witness to major events in the life of the Ritz Ballroom. By doing so, it is hoped that a better understanding will be made of how significant the Ritz was, and still is, to those generations of "happy dancers."

*Direct transcriptions of newspaper articles are indicated with an asterisk. In some cases errors have been corrected and bracketed. Some repetition exists in articles.

JCW

Foreword

by Les Brown, Jr.

When I was a child, I became aware that my father always went to work at night. Most of my friends' fathers went to work during the day so I asked dad what he did for a living. He told me he was a bandleader and the band was called "Les Brown & the Band of Renown" and they played music for dancers in ballrooms. I didn't quite grasp what that meant so I pestered him until he finally agreed to let me come and see him at work.

That was the beginning of a love affair with not only the music but the atmosphere that I saw in those ballrooms. It was a magical experience, all those people dancing and enjoying themselves and the sound of the instruments coming from the bandstand. I thought "this is for me."

In 1946, the band joined Bob Hope and we moved to Hollywood where Bob did his weekly radio show. The band also became a regular at one of the premiere ballrooms in the country, the Hollywood Palladium. I practically grew up in that wonderful "art deco" building. Every weekend I would go with dad and stand and watch the band and the people. Not too long after that I made my debut at the Palladium playing a clarinet duet with dad. I was hooked on performing.

Dad and the band were very fortunate in that the Bob Hope radio and later television show kept the band in California for most of the year. Every summer they would go on the road and tour the great ballrooms throughout the country for twelve weeks. When I was fifteen dad took me out on my first summer tour and I was able to see all the ballrooms, big and small, in all the cities before they closed a few years later.

All the big cities had great showplace ballrooms. . . . The Meadowbrook in New Jersey, The Casa Loma in St. Louis, Elitch Gardens in Denver, The Aragon in Chicago and, of course, The Ritz. What wonderful palaces they were and what a terrific time to grow up and be able to see and be a part of those times.

It is my sincere hope that all who see this book will experience the history and the warmth and good fellowship that was so much a part of that time. To use a word that is used, in my opinion, much too casually today it was truly *awesome!*

Les Brown, Sr., and his Band of Renown regularly played in Bridgeport at both the Ritz and Pleasure Beach ballrooms. One of the most popular bands, his orchestra survived the demise of most other big bands. In fact, in 1996 the Guinness Book of Records awarded Les Brown the distinction of being the leader of the longest continuous running musical organization in the history of pop music. The band continues to add to its legacy today under the leadership of his son, Les Brown, Jr.

Les Brown

Les Sr. onstage with band and dancers at the Hollywood Palladium

Prologue

For most of the twentieth century thousands of dance halls and ballrooms were scattered across America, each an oasis of fun and enjoyment. Some were truly palaces, others, simple and plain. But what they all had in common was being magnets for those who wanted to have fun, share quality interactions, and enjoy fine music.

Author Jack Behrens in his book, *Big Bands & Great Ballrooms*, states: *Older Americans will tell you 'you had to be there to feel the excitement.' No different, I suppose, than today when events or special occasions create more than the usual emotional tug. In the days of the big bands, however, it was a combination of feeling, the ambiance of the ballroom, the musical group and the special person you were with. It was magnetic and it usually sprang from the buzz of high school hallways, campus student unions or street corners prior to the special night. From the 1930s through the twilight of the ballroom days in the 1960s, the get-away-from-it-all feeling was spontaneous when a big band was coming to a favorite spot close by.*

With only radio and primitive early recordings available to lovers of music, each of which lacked the fidelity of live music, people relished being in the presence of a large live big band or orchestra in a place where they could hold someone close and dance the night away.

In Bridgeport, Connecticut, the two dance palaces of note were the Pleasure Beach Ballroom, located on an island just offshore, and the fabled Ritz Ballroom. Dancers would enjoy the Ritz in the winter and then retreat to Pleasure Beach in the summer where cool sea breezes blew through the gigantic dance facility, making even the hottest of summer nights bearable to the energetic dancers. Some city theaters such as the Lyric showcased name bands for concerts and drew crowds, but most people longed to dance to the music, thus flocking to the ballrooms.

While the Pleasure Beach Ballroom was larger, it was the Ritz Ballroom that had a certain magic that was felt by patrons. The Ritz, in actuality, *was* quite large, with some comparing it to an airplane hanger. But, as large as it was, there was also a coziness about the place. Whether it was the charm and attractiveness of the setting, the style and high standards set by management, or simply its welcoming and comfortable atmosphere, the Ritz attracted the crowds, sometimes thousands in an evening, and some from as far away as New York and Massachusetts.

It is the story of the Ritz Ballroom that this volume focuses on without any disrespect to its sister dance hall on the island. For the Ritz has a unique and wonderfully enchanting story to be told, a story I hope I have done justice to as I pieced together its history through numerous news articles and clippings, photos and artwork, and hours listening to the memories of many who spent years taking trolley, bus, or car to frequent their palace of fun in Black Rock.

My interest and passion for the Ritz was sparked by my parents, Rosemary (Mercurio) and Howard Williams, who met at the Ritz and, like thousands of others, ended up becoming lifetime partners in marriage. Years later, in 1997, I began broadcasting a radio show called *The Ritz Ballroom* Sunday evenings on WICC 600AM. Dedicated to the music and memories of the Ritz, the show earned significant ratings, and enabled me to invite numerous guests, including notable bandleaders and singers of the era, as well as local former Ritz patrons, to share their remembrances. Now in its fifteenth year and renamed *At The Ritz!*, the weekly program continues to keep the Ritz name, legacy, and great music alive and available to both veteran music fans and younger admirers, many of whom are just discovering what the rest of us know so well about quality music.

Guy Lombardo

Over the years many callers shared their Ritz memories and added to my enthusiasm in creating a listening opportunity for those who remember happy dance days, miss the music they grew up on, and longed for a chance to remember the romance and relive the memories that meant so much to them. As a result of this interest in sharing their memories, and ongoing eager attendance at the many Ritz dances I have staged in the region, I felt compelled to document the story for posterity. This year is the fiftieth anniversary of the closing of the Ritz which makes this project all the more timely and melancholy, especially for those "happy dancers" still with us.

Having been rented out as a furniture store, the Ritz still had an office where owners Joseph Barry and George McCormack worked for all those many years. Dozens of framed photos, posters, and other memorabilia decorated the walls, each with its own story to tell and moment to remember. No one had the presence of mind to clean out the Ritz office when Breiner's Furniture moved in. After the subsequent demise of Joe Barry, the office and its contents remained silent, a tomb filled with memories and photos, files, records and documents. Thus it was that this precious archive of mementos sadly went up in flames as the tragic fire erased all physical remnants of the beloved dance hall.

Without such a resource, your writer put a call out to former "Ritzies" (defined as loyal attendees for several decades). Local residents were invited to several public gatherings to share their personal memories and memorabilia, adding to the research that was done to make the story of the Ritz as complete as possible. Various celebrities who were radio show guests readily recalled visiting and performing at the Ritz. In addition, I have also drawn from the first-hand stories of Adele Barry Chappel, daughter of Ritz co-founder Joseph Barry, and the late Joey Zelle, leader of the Casa Ritz Orchestra. I cherish my ongoing friendship with Adele and value having gotten to know Joey whose thick scrapbook was invaluable in my research.

Of course, the resources of the Bridgeport Public Library and local historians along with extensive Internet research helped fill in details and added interesting revelations.

Collectively, the above resources and firsthand recollections helped to enhance the story of that big white building in the Black Rock section of Bridgeport, which stood for over four decades. Those who read this book will undoubtedly comment on various things left out, personal remembrances or details imbedded in their memories that may have been overlooked or missed. To those individuals I offer the last few pages that are dedicated to be a home for their own memorabilia, journal entries, and photos.

Part history, but mostly a pictorial scrapbook, *Home of Happy Dancers* is intended to be a keepsake to be shared with children and grandchildren who will never know the magic, the music, and the majesty of gliding upon that marvelous dance floor, under the red and white tapestry, surrounded by hundreds of other dancers as the music played on.

Benny Goodman

Bob Eberly

Anita O'Day

Chapter One

The Early Years

Paul Whiteman Orchestra, Circa 1920

If those floorboards could talk what stories they would tell. Punished by years of surface abuse, and suffering two relocations, the maple planks withstood decades of use, but were also witness to some of the happiest times of several generations of southern Connecticut residents. For those floorboards were the dance floor of the Ritz Ballroom, but not at the beginning—let me explain.

A few centuries ago, when Native Americans roamed the foothills and forests of what is now the Trumbull section of Fairfield County, there was a clearing in the woods where many footpaths led. A bucolic setting, with rushing water and, tall hardwood trees and conifers, this was a tranquil, serene place where those local Native Americans found peace and solitude. No one knows how far back this region attracted area inhabitants, but things began to change as much of the southern Connecticut lands became invaded by settlers during the 1700s and 1800s.

The industrial revolution of the mid-1800s was also a time when mass transit first came into vogue. Trains and trolleys started to crisscross the region. But without destinations, no one would take a trolley; therefore, the trolley companies created some destination attractions. That is how Savin Rock on the shore in West Haven came into being and how another pleasant spot—none other than the old Native American hangout described above—became what was known as Parlor Rock.

Beverly White, vocalist with Claude Hopkins Orchestra

Parlor Rock consisted of various buildings that housed recreational activities. One such building was a roller skating rink, the floor of which was built by felling maple and other hardwood trees in the vicinity. Plank by plank, the floor was born, destined to be used and abused by millions of people over its eighty-year lifespan.

So, people took the trolleys to Parlor Rock, enjoyed the activities, and all was well. By 1900, the park became a bit less popular and several of the buildings were to be sold off. The skating rink was closed, but an entrepreneur saw value in the floor and bought it to be moved and used as the floor for a new roller-skating rink in Bridgeport. This new venue, the Brooklawn Skating Pavilion, was located on the entire city block of Brooklawn and Capital Avenues. A turn of the century structure, the pavilion was the host to legions of skaters and the wonderful hardwood floor continued to serve its patrons well.

Some fifteen years later, the rink changed hands. Two hoofers by the name of Joseph Barry and George McCormack had another vision for the pavilion. They joined forces and bought the roller-skating rink, only to make one significant change—no more skates. The pavilion became a dance hall and flourished throughout the years on either side of World War I. And, of course, the magnificent planks of maple began to feel the soft feet of dancers who reveled in the pleasant comfort of the warm wood below them.

Claude Hopkins Orchestra

"Smiling Frankie Carle" the lad who knows more about the piano than the makers. He is one of the cleverest pianists in the dance music field, and his flying fingers can do some incredible feats on the keys.

Did I say flourished? Indeed, after a number of years the Brooklawn Dance Pavilion became too small for the throngs of those who frequented it, so Messrs. Barry and McCormack realized they needed more room, and began looking around. Their search brought them to property in the Black Rock section of the Park City, adjacent to Ash Creek. A deal was struck and plans were underway for a new dance palace, larger than the pavilion, and planned in such a fashion so that it could accommodate huge crowds of dancers. Named after the famous Ritz in New York City, the Ritz Ballroom started to rise at 3243 Fairfield Avenue. And those fabulous floorboards, now mellow and primed for more service to dancers, were moved once again.

Disaster! In moving the floor the truck carrying the load broke down on Brooklawn Avenue. However, a happy ending ensued, and the floor was moved, intact, once again to its final home in the brand-new Ritz Ballroom.

Adele Barry Chappel, daughter of Joseph Barry, has vivid memories of the Ritz's construction. "My father gave me payroll money for the workman from time to time," Adele recalls, "and as a young girl I had this important mission that everyone depended on. The workmen were always happy to see me!"

Built as a long rectangular structure, with a sunken dance floor and railed perimeter promenade surrounding the dance floor, the design of the Ritz was perfect for unobstructed viewing and dancing. Decorated with multicolored ceiling tapestries, and with carved design work on the supporting columns, the room was wonderfully spacious. The bandstand occupied a middle section of one of the room's large sides and was opposite the entrance door—a perfect greeting for those who paid their

Lionel Hampton

money to enter what eventually was to become one of Bridgeport's most popular and famous entertainment venues.

On one end of the ballroom was the coatroom, on the other a soda fountain. Cushioned benches, tables, and chairs were located all around the room, a few steps higher than the dance floor and behind the railed promenade, for resting and viewing the other dancers and orchestra. On the lower level was the changing room for the band, a sign painting shop, a grill for hot dogs and hamburgers, and the restrooms.

Such was the vision and setting created by Barry and McCormack that would greet throngs of "happy dancers" that would eventually number in the tens of thousands over four decades!

Buddy Morrow

George Shearing

Chapter Two

Bridgeport Post Centennial, February 7, 1983

Almost Everyone 'Put on the Ritz' by Deborah Rick

Photo by Bridgeport's Corbit Photographic Studios, courtesy of Bridgeport History Center

Ask just about anyone what a night "at the Ritz" was like and they'll probably sing you a song that will dance in your heart. "It was a ballroom that was a pleasure to go in," said William Ratzenberger, Jr., a trumpet player with the Ritz house bands. "You never had to worry about getting into any arguments with anybody. It was very well run. . . it was *the* place in New England," Ratzenberger recalled.

There probably isn't a "Ritzie" who doesn't have some fond memories of the ballroom days, when you forgot your cares, dressed up like you were going to a wedding and danced the night away—to some of the nation's greatest bands.

That glorious era strutted in because of an innovation made by two Bridgeport vaudeville hoofers. The ballroom's colorful history traces back to 1910, when George S. McCormack and Joseph R. Barry took the first step and opened the Brooklawn Pavilion. "Barry was always a showman," recalled Adele Chappel of Weston, daughter of the show business entrepreneur. Barry grew up on the east side of Bridgeport. As a youngster he worked as a newsboy with the company serving the New Haven Railroad. He became known as the "king" of the New York office, according to Mrs. Chappel, because he had one of the largest routes.

RITZ BALLROOM, for four decades the rendezvous for the romance-seekers and practically every one of the nation's top dance bands, closes its doors as a dance hall on Jan. 1, 1962 and reopens the following month as a furniture store.

Barry and McCormack met through stage experiences. Barry was a hoofer when he was introduced to McCormack, also a dancer on the Bridgeport circuit. The two hit it off and became friends. As Mrs. Chappel tells it, McCormack made Barry a business proposition one day. He approached Barry as he was ready to board the train to New York. The old Brooklawn Skating Rink was up for sale. Barry hadn't even seen the place, but he knew where it was, and because it met the qualifications for an amusement business, he offered his bank book to McCormack.

Servicing the dance and music loving fans of this vicinity continuously for the past 45 years and still going strong.

In May 1910, the partners secured the deal and became owners of the rink. They transformed it into a dance hall that became known as the Brooklawn Pavilion. It was on the corner of Brooklawn and Capitol Avenues, occupying the entire block bounded by Laurel and Cleveland Avenues. The Brooklawn dance house was the scene of many benefit dances and drives, and patriotic events during World War I. As it increased in popularity, the hall became too small. After 13 years the partners decided it was time to move. They scouted the Bridgeport area to find a location that would allow patrons to reach the dance hall by trolley. They chose a spot on Fairfield Avenue near the Fairfield town line.

GILMAN STEET, looking West, Black Rock's largest office building . . . the Frougt-Beverly block is pictured. Note large tree . . . as it is a traffic hazard, its removal has been on the agenda of the Black Rock Civic and Business Men's Club for many years.

Looking West. COURTLAND AVENUE on the left and DAVIDSON STREET on the right. The Ritz Ballroom is in left background.

POLAND STREET, looking East. Conspicuously on the left is Mack Motors. Right foreground shows Ray Arnold Company.

Black Rock neighborhood as you approach the Ritz Ballroom on Fairfield Avenue.

The maplewood dance floor from the Brooklawn Pavilion was moved out in two pieces. The transporting took place during a snowstorm, according to Mrs. Chappel. She said it tied up traffic for three days. McCormack was given a ticket and fined $50 for impeding traffic.

In March 1923, the Ritz Ballroom was born; it was located at 3243 Fairfield Avenue, just before Ash Creek. The Vincent Lopez Orchestra played for the gala opening. The $50,000 dance palace featured magnificent panels, mural decorations, ceiling draperies, crystal chandeliers with rose lights, thickly carpeted promenades, and spacious retiring rooms. The dance floor was built up of three layers of wood, which according to Mrs. Chappel, was like dancing on satin. There was also a soda fountain. The downstairs' smoking lounge, a typically Victorian amenity, was converted some years later into a grille, where dancers taking a breather could get hamburgers, hot dogs, and coffee. In time, a roofless Starlit Promenade was added. No liquor was ever served or allowed on the premises.

The admission price for an evening's dance was 15 cents at the Pavilion. It increased to 50 cents at the Ritz and went up to as much as $2.50 when some of the name bands were playing.

The Ritz was in full swing four nights a week. The polka and modern dances were featured on Wednesdays, and the square dance and waltz on Thursdays. The house bands (the William Malone Band and the Casa Ritz Orchestra) played on Saturdays. Sundays and holidays were the big nights, when the biggest name bands came.

During the five decades the Ritz was in existence the ballroom saw many changes. The Depression years were a challenge. Barry decided that one way to fight the problem was to make Thursday night "Prosperity Night." The admission price was reduced from 50 cents to 25 cents. The bargain price was an instant success.

Then the "big bands" were the rage, and the Ritz was swept by the craze. The names that played the Ritz in those days were big ones—Benny Goodman, Louis Armstrong, Count Basie, Tommy and Jimmy Dorsey, Horace Heidt, Artie

Shaw, Gene Krupa, Duke Ellington, Vaughn Monroe, Guy Lombardo, Les Brown, Harry James, Woody Herman, Vincent Lopez, Glenn Miller, Rudy Vallee, Fletcher Henderson, Chick Webb, Will Osborne, and Lionel Hampton. People came from all over to hear them.

Through the late 30s and into the 40s big bands reigned supreme. But World War II cut into the dance boom somewhat. With so many men in the service, women were left with few dancing partners. But after 1945, when the men returned, there was a rebirth of the dance hall—a short-lived one as it turned out. There was a growing lack of interest among young people. Television and automobiles were the new rage. There was more money around, and there were new places to spend it.

Then in 1948, McCormack died, and Barry later bought full ownership of the Ritz. He purchased his partner's half share from Mrs. Mary A. McCormack.

The Ritz tried to keep up with the changing times. Through the years the ballroom was rented out for social functions, including beauty pageants, banquets, proms, class nights, testimonials, and even some wedding receptions. But these rentals couldn't keep the ballroom in operation, and other new interests spelled its doom.

In 1961, in what he called his saddest decision, Barry granted a 10-year lease to Breiner Furniture Co. The furniture outlet did not move there until 1962, allowing the Ritz to go out with its traditional New Year's Eve dance. The fabulous Ritz era was swept into history on New Year's Eve, 1961, when couples jammed the hall to dance there for the last time.

The Ritz may have been "the" place to go, but it wasn't the only place to go dancing. Through the years, other ballrooms sprung up and became the summer homes of the Ritz. Because of sweltering heat here during the summer months—there wasn't much air conditioning around in those days—the Ritz shut down in June. The dancing shifted to other places such as the Pleasure Beach Ballroom.

For about five years during the 1930s, McCormack and Barry were the managing lessees of Pleasure Beach Ballroom, according to Mrs. Chappel. They also were managing lessees of the dance pavilion at Roton Point, South Norwalk; the Playland Casino in Rye, N.Y.; and the Pietche Tea Gardens in Peach Lake, N.Y. The same policies and ideals that the owners applied to the Ritz were applied to these ballrooms.

Barry died in 1962. Not only did an era end then, but during the next decade the last concrete memories were reduced to ashes, as both the Ritz and Pleasure Beach Ballrooms were swept away by spectacular fires. In June 1970, the one-time "Dance Fairyland of Bridgeport" burned to the ground. The fire that swept Breiner's furniture store was the end of the former Ritz Ballroom. In May 1973, fire swept the city-owned Pleasure Beach Ballroom, burning the 53-year-old landmark to the ground.

But for many, the good old memories linger. "It was the kind of fun you can't capture today," Mrs. Chappel said. "Everyone knew how to dance. You danced to the rhythms and bounced all over the world."

Chapter Three

Bridgeport Post, September 17, 1945

27 Injured at Ritz Dance as Promenade Collapses

Vaughn Monroe

Injured last night when a section of the promenade in the rear of the Ritz Ballroom collapsed and plunged many of them eight feet to the ground amid debris, five persons were still under treatment in St. Vincent's hospital today and 22 others were recovering in their homes following treatment, as insurance investigators visited the scene.

Witnesses said about 100 of the dancers attending a performance by Vaughn Monroe's orchestra were on the promenade porch during the usual 10:30 intermission when a 12-foot square section of the flooring at the western end sagged suddenly and collapsed without warning.

SEVERAL FALL TO THE GROUND

Several persons plunged through the opening and landed on the ground below, many succeeded in scrambling out of the dancer zone, and others clung to handholds on the main building until they were rescued.

George S. McCormack, co-owner of the ballroom, and Joseph Barry, said today the promenade structure had been examined last December by an insurance agency and was in "sound condition" at that time. He estimated damage to the flooring at $250 and said repairs will be started as soon as possible.

BUILDING INSPECTED

Building Inspector Bernard J. McKeivey said he and Fire Chief Martin J. Hayden had inspected the entire ballroom a year ago, but did not find it necessary to suggest any repairs at that time.

Mr. McCormack said the collapse began at a point where the promenade rests on one of a number of supporting concrete columns and that subsequent inspection showed some of the heavy timbers laid on the columns to support the flooring were in a rotted condition.

"JITTERBUGS" WARNED

"A group of youngsters were jumping up and down on the flooring and were warned to stop by one of the special policeman," the ballroom owners said. "Minutes later a section 12 feet square started to collapse and a large number of people inside the ballroom, thinking a fight had started, ran out onto the porch. The rotted condition of the supporting planks is probably a result of dampness and occasional flood tides during which the water rises to the lower portion of the promenade."

A special policeman reported that a number of "jitter-bugs" were jumping up and down on the wooden flooring before the section at the west end of the promenade gave way.

Sgt. Charles E. Wakeman, on desk duty at the Third Precinct police station, received first notification of the accident at 10:43 p.m. through a telephone call from a man who said he heard sounds of breaking glass and people screaming at the Ritz. Sgt. Wakeman notified Robert Delaney, dispatcher in the radio room at police headquarters, who summoned the city ambulance and sent radio cars into the scene.

Police and Doctors Frank Riccio and Frederick Rosner, of Emergency Hospital, were kept busy treating the injured and both city ambulances were pressed into service to take the more seriously injured to the hospital. Others were treated at the scene.

Dr. Stephen V. Pastor of 3063 Fairfield Avenue, who has offices near the Ritz, also aided until called back to his office when three Newtown residents appeared for treatment for shock and bruises. They did not reveal their names.

Police took immediate charge upon arrival under the direction of Capt. George A. Washburn. Later, Supt. John A. Lyddy arrived on the scene.

TAKEN TO THE HOSPITAL

The most seriously injured, all taken to St. Vincent's Hospital and remaining there overnight were:

Irene Plaudelt, 24, 801 Lafayette Street, possible fracture of the right shoulder.

Joe Maciwousky, 18, of 291 Coram Avenue, Shelton, possible back injuries.

William Carpenter, 19, of 390 East Main Street, possible fracture of pelvis.

Benito Gallucci, 16, of 581 East Main Street, possible fracture of the right shoulder and right leg.

Adele Petrusaitis, 23, of 11 Summer Street, possible fracture of the left ribs.

OTHERS TREATED

Others treated at the hospital and sent home include:

Pearl Moran, 18, of 143 Jennings Road, Fairfield, puncture wound of the left ankle and abrasions of the left knee.

Where 27 at Ritz dance were injured

Doris Santora, 25, of 68 Randall Avenue, abrasions of the left leg.

Paula Santora, 21, of 68 Randall Avenue, abrasions of the left leg and chin.

Cora Daros, 34, of 28 Thompson Street, possible fracture of the right ankle and abrasions of the chin.

Ruth Lyons, 16, of 69 Washington Street, Waterbury, abrasions, both legs.

Doris Sicard, 17, of 201 Willow Street, Waterbury, abrasions of left ankle and leg.

Catherine Lasky, 15, of 489 King's Highway, Fairfield, abrasions of both legs.

Anna DeLuca, 18, of 218 Housatonic Avenue, scraped right leg and elbow.

Jean Moran, 15, of 143 Jennings Road, Fairfield, treated for shock.

Leona Pandora, 26, of 152 Norman Street, possible fracture of the left ankle.

Alexander Trabka, 17, of 91 Caroline Street, Derby, fracture of the left arm.

TREATED AT SCENE

Those treated at the Ritz were:

Mrs. Kinonary, 268 Eastlawn Road, Fairfield; Michael Mangicoti, 114 Grove Street, Waterbury; Louis Procopian, 56 West Liberty Street, Waterbury; R. Staellutto, 50 Meadow Street, Norwalk; D. Knapp, 60 Staples Street; Leo Baker, 2310 Main Street; Al Barker, 2310 Main Street; Mary Mihok, 39 Carroll Street; Helen Hibbard, 80 Howe Street, New Haven; Sydney Zolot, 86 Scranton Street, New Haven; Albino Pannolla, 61 George Street, East Haven; Louis Padolecchia, 114 Grove Street, Waterbury.

After the mishap, the dance program continued in the ballroom.

Hal McIntyre

Tex Beneke

Chapter Four

Bridgeport Post, October 31, 1948

Ray Colonari, Band Fan as a Boy, Named Assistant Manager of Ritz by Rocky Clark

Harry James at the Ritz

Ray Colonari, who collected records and made the acquaintance of popular bandleaders when he was a student at Bassick High School, began making his hobby pay off when he returned from the war. And today, as the climax, comes the announcement of his appointment as assistant manager of the Ritz Ballroom.

The ballroom, owned by Joseph Barry and Mrs. George McCormack, is one of the oldest and most successful in New England. Founded by Messrs. McCormack and Barry, it had been operated by them continually until Mr. McCormack's death during the past years.

Colonari, who has been working as a freelance disc jockey for Station WNAB, is a native of Bridgeport. He was born April 22, 1919, the son of former policeman Michael Colonari who is now employed by the Post Publishing Company.

Though not a musician himself, Ray has been a rabid follower of popular bandleaders and vocalists since his school days at Black Rock and Bassick High, from which he graduated in 1937. Before entering the Army in 1943, he worked at Howland's and the Bullard Company—spending his surplus earnings on recordings of his favorite stars.

Ray Colonari

When he entered the service, Colonari received nationwide publicity for his complete collection of Bing Crosby records. He had met and cultivated the friendship of Bing during Crosby's visits to the East.

He served in the C-B-I theater of war and did his first microphone work running a GI record show for the Armed Forces Radio Service in Burma.

Joe Barry (right) owner of the Ritz Ballroom was honored in 1959 by the Bridgeport Elks at a "Joe Barry Night" in the Elks Club, Fairfield, in celebration of his 50th year in show business and his 49th year as a member of the Elks. Lester C. Burdick (left), a dance partner of Mr. Barry, back in 1909, presents a plaque to his old-time sidekick. Ray Colonari, center, was chairman for the event.

Following his discharge, he was the guest of this writer on "Rock 'n' Rhythm" to present a typical GI record show for WNAB listeners. The WNAB management was impressed with his performance, and Ray soon had his own program. "Ray's Record Review," on the station's Saturday schedule.

His radio activities increased last season when he became the announcer for WNAB's "remote" broadcasts from the Ritz Ballroom where his knowledge of bands impressed the proprietors. Yesterday they announced his appointment as assistant manager to Mr. Barry.

Married to the former Ruth Smith, he is the father of two children—Robert, five years old, and Nancy, four months.

His first project on his new job will be a "Teen-Time Dance" for teen-agers tomorrow night from 8 to 11 p.m. Ronny Rommel's Collegiate Sextet will provide the music.

Chapter Five

Union News, Circa 1950

Ray Colonari

Ray Colonari

Watching a young man with a lot of talent rapidly advance in his chosen field has been the pleasure of your reporter and all of Bridgeport during the past two years. The individual is Ray Colonari who holds the post now of manager at the popular Ritz Ballroom on Fairfield Avenue. To trace Ray's career is to notice a steady forward progress and we would like to do that for you as we believe Ray is a shining example that a fellow with a lot on the ball can forge a success out of music, even here in Bridgeport, believe it or not.

While in the army over in Burma, Ray started a disc jockey show for the Armed Forces Radio outlet and it proved to be a definite success. Upon his return home, and back to civilian life, Ray had the good fortune to talk this over with Rocky Clark, radio editor of the Post, and the fellow who runs the "Rockin' Rhythm" show each week on WNAB. As a result, Ray appeared as a guest one night and put on a typical recorded Armed Forces show such as he had done while in the service. This caused a lot of fine comment around WNAB and, as a result, Ray became one of the local station's disk jockeys with a fine show each week. Titled "Ray's Record Review," the program became a definite hit and, showing his interest in local musicians, Ray gave many a local band fine plugs, plus having several local leaders featured on his show. These included, among others, Ronny Rommel, Joey Zelle, Ed Graff, and Jack Still. And Ray also managed to interview several top name leaders on his show whenever they were in town. To understand how Ray did this we have to go back a few years.

Ray was always interested in music, and can still play the piano (with the shortage of piano men, he should have stuck to it) although this isn't generally known. Ray always managed to find time to listen to bands catching all remotes until the stations went off the air. As time went by, Ray started to collect records and, at the present, he has one of the largest collections in these parts. In fact, his collection of rare Crosby platters promoted an Associated Press feature story. Ray always travelled to catch bands and, even in his youth, was the accepted authority on all bands. Ray admits he was a constant nuisance to his family and not popular on a date as his time was spent talking to the musicians, with very little time allowed for dancing. But all this did pay off when Ray assumed his radio show. Musicians remembered him and went out of their way to give him a hand.

Ray then took over the record department at the Black Rock Appliance Co. and turned a lot of his efforts to the local musicians. He ran several block parties, arranged for band appearances on the March of Dimes shows and worked with local leaders. His objective, then, as now, was to publicize the fact that Bridgeport musicians were deserving of a wider range of appreciation.

The crowning point of his career, admits Ray, was the day the opportunity came to become associated with the master showman, Joe Barry, of the Ritz Ballroom. He started there in 1948 and now finds himself up to his ears in music, both with local leaders and the name bands that the Ritz features each week. He loves every minute of it and his early interest and knowledge has proved of invaluable help to him. He is doing what he likes and that is the most important thing in any job.

To us who have known Ray a good many years, it has been a real thrill to note his steady progress up the ladder. He started as a fan following the bands, became a disc jockey, then ran a record shop, and finally rose to rate the job at the Ritz. We know that from here Ray's progress will be just as steady. His future should be brilliant and it will be well-deserved. A nice guy who is only too happy to do anyone a favor, Ray holds the respect and well-wishes of all in Local 63. So, good luck, Ray Colonari, and we can only say, it couldn't happen to a nicer guy.

Harry James

Helen O'Connell

Helen Young

Sammy Kaye

Chapter Six

Union News, September 1950

Joey Zelle

Joey Zelle

Taking over the spotlight in this month's review of our local bandleaders is a young man well known to local dancers, fellow musicians, and practically everyone in the town. By now you may have guessed his name—it is Joey Zelle, maestro of the "swellegant" crew which holds the title of "house band" at the popular Ritz Ballroom on Fairfield Avenue.

Joey is rated as one of the better trumpet players in this area, but really takes bows for the very fine arrangements he turns out. All of the tunes in the Casa Ritz book were penned by Joey, and it is needless to say how wonderful they sound. Here is a young man who not only stands in front of his band and directs, but puts down all the notes that the band plays to be directed.

Leader of the band

Getting his career under way, Joe started with Ronny Rommel as a horn man in the Ritz band way back in 1942. After a season he left Ronny and joined forces with the Vinnie Wilson big band which held forth at Pleasure Beach Ballroom. He left Vinnie's band only to return again following stints with Frank Dailey at Laddin's Terrace and Eddie Antalick at Lenny's Rainbow Room. This time Vinnie Wilson's band took over the spot at the Rustic Cabin in New Jersey where Joey did all the arranging for the band and was featured as horn man. What followed was work with Kenny Sargeant's band in Memphis, Tenn. until he returned home to Bridgeport to form his own band. Eventually McCormack and Barry of the Ritz talked with Joey, urged him to cut the size of his band, and then gave him the assignment as house band at this popular ballroom.

Joey's instrumentation included five saxes, three rhythm, himself on horn, plus two vocalists and the band really caught on with the dancing public. After a very successful year, they won the WNAB band poll. In honor of this, McCormack and Barry ran a testimonial dance to honor the band, and "Joey Zelle night" drew over 1900 people to the Ritz. This is really a tribute to Joey especially when it happens in Bridgeport. Anytime the dancing public here locally will turn out in droves to honor a local band, it is really stupendous news. But they did it for Joey and the tribute was really deserving. And Joey has started another first during the season by airing over WNAB direct from the Ritz each Saturday, and having his weekly air show listed as one of the top programs to be carried by the local station.

Holiday Trumpet Time

When we talked to Joey to get some material for this resumé, one of the things that remained with us, was the

Man with the trumpet

fact that Joey insisted we mention the people who he feels have helped to make all of his good fortune possible. He feels none of it would have been possible but for the help of Joe Barry, the late George McCormack, Mrs. McCormack, and Ray Colonari. Their guidance has been a wonderful thing for Joey and has really helped in putting his band across. Joey also wants to thank Rocky Clark and Fred Russel of the *Post*; Harry Neigher of the *Herald*, and engineers and staff of Stations WNAB, WICC, and WLIZ, all to take a bow for their wonderful work and stories about the band, making the dancing public conscious of it.

To sum up, Joey Zelle is merely to mention the fine things he has done in the past, and to use that as a criterion, to know he will continue to do many more in the future. He's a swell guy heading a mighty fine band that should go on to new heights as the years roll by. Congratulations to Joey Zelle, our "Band Leader of the Month."

The original nine-piece band with vocalists Helen Shaw and Manning Cox

Larry Gray

Ray Eberle

Chapter Seven

Bridgeport Herald, June 14, 1952

Old Times with Joe Hurley

It's 1922 and there are McCormack and Barry on the steps of the old Brooklawn Pavilion

The kids of this fast-moving day and age ought to get a kick out of this column—Especially those who love to trip the light fantastic. If you were to go back some 40 years, kids, you'd find your "old man" tripping that so called "light fantastic" at the old Brooklawn Pavilion, owned by Joe Barry and George "Pinch" McCormack at Brooklawn and Capitol Avenues, in what was then known as the swanky section of Brooklawn.

The dance pavilion, reconverted roller skating rink, was almost directly opposite the exclusive Brooklawn Club, where golf was played only by a few old duffers who had a lot of money and didn't know what else to do with themselves for relaxation.

The only means of transportation to old Brooklawn was the trolley car. You boarded the Stratfield trolley at Main and Fairfield, and by the time the old clang clang reached Brooklawn, if you were lucky, you had a least the first four or five dances booked for the evening.

Some of the poor gals took double punishment in those days—You stepped on their feet because of the crowded condition of the trolley and mutilated their tootsies a bit more when you took them out on the floor. There were only two dance numbers in those days, an old-fashioned waltz or a fast one step! The fox trot was just about being born with only the best of dancers attempting its intricate movement.

LAST TROLLEY HURRIED ALONG ON GOOD NIGHTS

If you went out to Brooklawn on a chilly Fall evening or in the Winter you found four round-bellied stoves trying to keep the place warm. If a gal sat out a couple of dances she was in danger of freezing to death.

When McCormack and Barry ran out of coal, they would put a red lantern in the stove to give you the idea there was a roaring fire inside. You danced around a square platform set up in the middle of the rectangular floor. One of the most popular numbers was that old-fashioned waltz when they dimmed the lights and used a spotlight. You danced away from the spotlight if you were a poor dancer or had a special little message to tell the gal you were dancing with. If you took a gal home from the dance and she lived within a mile of the pavilion you walked home because it took you at least an hour to say "Good Night" and by that time the last trolley had left.

Sometimes you got a ride home with a milkman coming down from Fairfield Woods or Easton. When World War I came along in 1917, the Brooklawn Pavilion was about the most popular spot in town and the boys who enlisted in the old 26th Yankee Division or the 56th Coast Artillery began to appear in uniforms after they marched off to war and came home on leave. Many of the Brooklawn patrons of that day founded their war, romance, and marriage at the old pavilion—After the war, Brooklawn was still the mecca for the returning heroes. It was not until 1926 [1923] that McCormack and Barry opened up their Ritz dance hall in Black Rock.

NOTE: McCormack and Barry's establishment was listed in the 1913 City Directory as Brooklawn Dancing Pavilion.

Chapter Eight

Bridgeport Sunday Post, May 22, 1955

Ritz Cancels Rock 'N' Roll Band

"Fats" Domino

A dance scheduled for the Ritz Ballroom tonight with the band of "Fats" Domino, has been cancelled by Joseph Barry, proprietor of the ballroom, because of inferences that "Rock 'n' Roll" dances might be featured.

Mr. Barry said he cancelled the dance voluntarily because of a recent police ban on Rock 'n' Roll parties after a riotous dance in the New Haven area.

Supt. John A. Lyddy and Sgt. Richard Svertesky of the Police Youth Bureau both called to inquire about the dance, Mr. Barry said, but the decision to cancel it was entirely his.

The superintendent said last night that he had no intention of asking Mr. Barry to cancel the dance, even though there were strong indications that Rock 'n' Roll dancing would appear on the band's program.

"The police department ban is on unsupervised dancing or dance parties which tend to have a demoralizing affect on teenagers, or for that matter, adults," the superintendent said. "Mr. Barry has operated a reputable dance ballroom for many years and I certainly respect his judgment in whatever bands he books or the dances he stages in his ballroom."

Mr. Barry said that he had planned to have four extra special policemen on duty at the dance tonight to insure an orderly dance party.

"I wasn't the least bit worried that the dance tonight would have been any the less orderly than any other dance in the ballroom, but I also have no wish to become involved in a controversial issue."

The Crewcuts

The Four Lads

The Beachcombers

Chapter Nine

Bridgeport Post, October 8, 1955

Ritz Manager Recalls His Career as Newspaper Boy 50 Years Ago

Casually-dressed Barry has vivid memories of his younger days

Today's observance of National Newspaper Day, which closes National Newspaper Week, brought keen memories to a member of the fraternity more than 50 years ago.

Joseph R. Barry, manager of the Ritz Ballroom during the last 45 years, began his successful career as a newsboy in the East Side at the age of 12.

While attending Barnum School, he carried three routes in his neighborhood. He would rise before dawn and deliver the Bridgeport morning paper. At 7 a.m. he would be at the railroad station to await the arrival of the New York papers and then deliver a New York route. In the afternoon, after school, he carried the *Farmer* and the *Bridgeport Post*.

EMPLOYED BY H. S. CHALLENGER

Mr. Barry was one of approximately 30 boys working for the late Howard S. Challenger out of his Crescent Avenue newsroom. This experience stood him in good stead when he applied for a newsboy job with the company serving the New Haven railroad at that time. He went on the railroad when he was 14 selling newspapers and magazines. Twice daily he rode between New Haven and New York.

Eventually he served in several capacities for the Union News company, finally becoming manager of that firm's Grand Central Terminal outlet.

Simultaneously he and George McCormack opened the Ritz Ballroom (Brooklawn Pavilion) in 1907 [1910] and were drawing approximately $100 a week in profits from the dance hall venture. He stayed on the railroad 23 years and during that time worked nights in the Ritz.

Among his happy memories are selling papers to Presidents Theodore Roosevelt and William Howard Taft, stage star Eva Tanguay and screen stars Douglas Fairbanks and Mary Pickford. Another happy day occurred when Harvard alumni invited him to serve them on a 13-car special train headed for Cambridge and the Yale-Harvard game.

Being a newspaper boy, he says, was a rich and rewarding experience and gave him an education as well.

Joseph R. Barry

Jimmy Dickens and his Country Boys

Chapter Ten

Bridgeport Post, Monday February 3, 1958

Snap Shots and Short Stories by Edward W. Plaisted

Diane Williams   Joseph Barry   Jack Still   John Still

QUESTION: WHAT IS YOUR FAVORITE NAME DANCE ORCHESTRA?

Pat Grant   Thomas R. Bruno   Jean M. Crosby   Helen M. Krolides

DIANE WILLIAMS, 118 Wheeler Avenue, vocalist:

"I think Les Brown's is the greatest to dance to because his arrangements are understandable and so much happens when he plays. His music isn't monotonous like Lawrence Welk. Les Brown is just great. That is the best way to sum it up."

JOE BARRY, 3243 Fairfield Avenue, ballroom operator:

"Guy Lombardo is the best dance band I have known in the 43 years I've been in this business. Guy's band is the one band where even the old folks get a kick out of dancing to. In fact, the last time Guy played here we were really packed."

JACK STILL, 127 Ronald Drive, Fairfield, orchestra leader:

"I like a lot of bands but Les Elgart and Lawrence Welk are tops in the dance music department. I'm sorry to see the poor attendance at local dances of late because if people continue to dance they will stay younger longer."

JOHN STLL, 327 Laurel Avenue, base player:

"I disagree with my brother Jack, somewhat because I like Guy Lombardo and Lawrence Welk. They play danceable music, and what's more, it's understandable music—the same type Jack plays. This rock 'n' roll junk has got to go. It just isn't music."

PAT GRANT, 3243 Fairfield Avenue, policeman:

"Guy Lombardo is the best band from the dancer's point of view. For music to listen to it's the original Jimmy Lunceford band. That's my opinion after watching 'em every week for the past 26 years at the Ritz. I think I like Lunceford overall also."

THOMAS R. BRUNO, 709 Queen Street, machinist:

"Guy Lombardo, because I think he makes for good, smooth dancing for older folks like myself. I've been attending dances at the Ritz and Pleasure Beach ballrooms for almost 26 years now and there truly isn't any sweeter music this side of heaven."

Jimmie Lunceford

JEAN M. CROSBY, 630 John Street, timekeeper:

"Xavier Cugat, because I love Latin American music. Cugat is the only orchestra that really gives the right treatment to the style of dancing music. Brother, someday I hope to retire and live on some Latin American island and just listen to this kind of music."

HELEN M. KROLIDES, 137 Hollister Street, Stratford:

"Guy Lombardo, because he plays such sweet, dreamy music for dancing that is so romantic. I don't like these so-called modern bands who play nothing but rock 'n' roll numbers because to me that isn't music. It may be OK for the kids, but give me Guy Lombardo any day."

Chapter Eleven

Sunday Herald, October 22, 1961

Famed Ritz Ballroom Leased; Will Become Furniture Store by Harry Neigher

Duke Ellington

The Ritz Ballroom, Bridgeport's most glorious landmark and last-remaining pleasure palace, is being converted into a furniture store.

The Ritz, bastion for two generations of romance-seekers, prom trotters, big band devotees and chicken and green pea testimonial dinner frequenters, will close its portals New Year's morning, 1962, with the last strains of *Auld Lang Syne*. A month later it will reopen as Breiner's Furniture Store.

Negotiations will be completed this coming week by Joseph R. Barry, president of Brooklawn Amusement Co, and sole operator of the Ritz Ballroom for the long-term leasing of his nationally famous dance emporium to Mitchell Breiner, head of the Breiner Furniture Co. on Hancock Avenue.

Breiner, compelled to move from his present location because of the redevelopment in the West Side, has persuaded Barry to turn the Ritz over to him. Terms of the 10-year lease will permit Breiner to convert the Ritz Ballroom into a furniture store and showroom.

Storybook romance fanciers will see the conversion of the Ritz Ballroom into a furniture stores as a natural evolution—from dancing feet to romance to engagement and marriage and the furnishing of a new home.

To thousands of grandmothers and grandfathers and their sons, daughters and grandchildren this news will conjure up fond memories of gay-hearted nights of frivolous dancing fun to the music of the nation's greatest dance bands.

To Joe Barry, who has watched jazz turn to swing and to rock 'n' roll, and kept the ballroom intact despite all those frenzied dance crazes as the Black Bottom, the Charleston, Bunny Hug, Big Apple, the Lindy Hop and the Bop—and now the Twists, giving up the Ritz is the closing chapter of a truly glamorous and exciting life.

To Joe Barry, whose canny operation of the Ritz through five decades has won him the title of dean of America's big ballroom impresarios, the decision to close down his storied dance hall was a difficult one. Barry, now 73 years old, was determined to continue the operation of the Ritz as a ballroom the rest of his life—and he never wanted it said that he stopped the music. His family counseled otherwise.

Barry retains ownership title to the Ritz Ballroom building and land, and is renting it to Breiner on a 10-year lease, with an option to renew the lease for another 10 years. He is also giving Breiner the first option to buy the Ritz Ballroom and land if and when he or his heirs decide to sell.

Breiner has long yearned to purchase the Ritz. He first approached Barry seven years ago, but Joe turned down his proposition. But last June, at daughter Carole's high school prom at the Ritz, Breiner again propositioned Barry, and found that Joe was now warmed up to the idea. By then, Barry's family had prevailed upon him to retire as titular head of America's foremost ballroom.

"I finally decided to accept Breiner's offer to rent the Ritz and let him turn it into a furniture showplace!" said Barry. "After 52 years in the ballroom business, getting to work at 10 a.m. and getting home at three or four the next morning, I guess I've had enough. Breiner will find me an ideal landlord—one he'll never see."

Barry's decision to lease the ballroom comes at a most propitious time for Breiner, for his present place of business, a three-story structure in the West End, has been acquired by the City of Bridgeport to make way for the West Side Redevelopment No. 1.

Joe Barry and George McCormack were mere boys back in 1910 when they conceived the idea of going into show business together. There were members of the A.B.C. Club, a hangout where kids of the East Side of Bridgeport with singing or dancing talent would rehearse and put on minstrel shows. Hundreds of kids paid admission to the Joe Barry Theater in the Barry woodshed. Joe had the most persistent fascination for show business and proved it by winning a state baton twirling championship in his teens—using a sawed broomstick for a baton. Then he won prizes as a dance hoofer, but had to sell newspapers on the trains to keep eating.

First teaming up as friends, young McCormack and Barry decided to go into the silent motion picture business, but changed their minds when they found they hadn't enough change in their pockets.

Then McCormack proposed they buy the Brooklawn Pavilion which was for sale. George used considerable persuasion and Joe agreed, thinking it was a skating rink they were buying. It wasn't until the night before they reopened the Pavilion on Memorial Day of 1910 that Joe Barry discovered he was in the dance business with George McCormack—and Joe's been in it ever since.

From that day in 1910, McCormack and Barry operated the Brooklawn for the dances and public soirees—from baby shows to Mardi-Gras carnivals—and during World War I the place hummed with patriotic endeavors such as war bond drives and benefit dances.

The daring young partners always wore evening clothes as they welcomed their customers, and when the crowds exited, they scrambled out of their tuxedos and into old clothes to clean the place up for the next night.

The dance hall was heated by four stoves and many a night when the coal ran out, a lighted red lantern was placed in each stove to give the impression of warmth and cheer.

The late Jack Spiedel and his orchestra provided most of the dance music in those early days, and on the slow or rainy nights is was Barry's job to say: "Sorry Jack, but we can only come across with a dollar apiece for the musicians tonight! And Jack Spiedel would invariably reply: "Of course it's Okay with me—but that fellow with the bass violin has to come all the way from Trumbull in a buggy, and he has to have money for the horse's oats. You can't expect the best bull fiddler in the country to carry the fiddle on his back those many miles—for a dollar!"

So Barry and McCormack would have to shell out another dollar.

For 13 years, from May 30, 1910, to September 22, 1923, Joe and Mac ran the Brooklawn. They worked hard, and they prospered. In 1923, they gave way to progress and the old Brooklawn Dancing Pavilion was no more. The Ritz Ballroom became their new venture. And the following news item from a Bridgeport newspaper that day in September 1923 recorded the historic event for posterity.

"George S. McCormack, of 1887 Fairfield Avenue, dance hall proprietor, was arrested on the charge of moving a section of the dance flooring from the Brooklawn Pavilion to the McCormack and Barry dance hall on Fairfield Avenue, near Ash Creek. He was fined $50 and costs in City Court. He went ahead with the moving of the flooring after being ordered to wait until midnight to do it."

Where was partner Joe Barry? Oh, he was right there, too, helping move the famous maple floor in four sections and placing it in the present Ritz Ballroom. But dapper George McCormack was the senior partner, so he took the rap in court.

Under Barry and McCormack, the Ritz Ballroom flourished and today it is rated as the foremost ballroom in New England. Through many decades of watching teenagers and adults doing everything from the Lambeth Walk to the jitterbug, Joe and Mac endured all types of weather and dance business recessions without permitting the standards and policies of their beloved Ritz Ballroom to be lowered one iota.

Keeping their Ritz free of roughhousing paid off handsomely. The Ritz survived when most of the other large ballrooms in the nation failed, and after four decades the Ritz became the last large operating ballroom in the nation. Soon it will be no more.

Barry, now 72, became the partner of Mrs. George McCormack after George's death in 1948, and later bought out her interest in the Ritz Ballroom.

Called the "oldest active ballroom impresario in America," Joe has worn his crown well. A man of tremendous vitality and with a great capacity for work, Barry could go on indefinitely if his family would let him. But they won't.

It was Joe, and his late partner, Mac, who brought the finest dance music to the people of Fairfield County for almost two generations . . . Rudy Vallee, Vaughn Monroe, Ozzie and Harriet Nelson, Paul Whiteman, the Dorsey Brothers, Maynard Ferguson, Mal Hallett, Larry Funk, Claude Hopkins, Isham Jones, Guy Lombardo and his Royal Canadians, to name a few.

Looking back, Barry recalls it was soon after he and Mac opened the Ritz that they gave Rudy Vallee his first break at the Ritz. It was one night in 1924 that Vallee burned up the Post Road from New Haven to Bridgeport to make his first bid as a crooner at the Ritz Ballroom, appearing with the Yale Collegians band, led by Sleepy Hall. Rudy then was just one of the side men tooting a saxophone and he was permitted to sing one number.

SIGNING OUT—Joseph R. Barry, who with the late George S. McCormack, opened the Ritz Ballroom in 1910 [1923], bids farewell to an operation no longer profitable to him. The popularity of the Ritz passed with the demise of the name bands.

The pleasant reaction he got from some of the Bridgeport girls convinced Vallee he had something, vocally. The following year, Rudy returned to the Ritz as leader of the same band, and made himself heard by crooning through a megaphone. This time the local gals went ga-ga over him and Vallee knew right then and there he was going places. And so did Ritz impresario Joe Barry. He got Rudy his first band bookings around New England.

It's no idle boast on Barry's part when he claims that he, more than any other man, should be credited as Vallee's discoverer and mentor. And even today, when Vallee is in this sector, he drops in or phones Barry and they chat for hours. Rudy Vallee holds the all-time attendance record for early Ritz Ballroom days. Vaughn Monroe holds the record for the more modern days at the Ritz, Barry recalls.

Charter member of Vallee's first fan club is Jolan Virag, now Mrs. George Antoniak, wife of the Black Rock printer.

Of course, ballroom dancing isn't what it used to be, says Joe. Take the new dance fad—the Twist. Barry wouldn't permit it on his dance floor now or any other such wiggling or squirming that masquerades as dancing. "Dating today is more or less an outdoor sport," says Joe. "Like the drive-in movies, where love has more privacy—and less waiting."

In the past few years, it's mostly banquets, prosperity night dances and proms at the Ritz, with an occasional name band during the winter months. But for many years the Ritz Ballroom was an integral part of Bridgeport's social life.

Breathes there a man or woman of this generation or of the generation before who doesn't have fond memories and nostalgia when the name Ritz Ballroom is mentioned. Thousands of romances began at the Ritz. And who doesn't have cherished memories of the Ritz with its Saturday and Sunday night dances with the great name bands in America—of its many proms and beauty contests.

Ray Anthony

Colorful Memories of The Ritz

THESE AND OTHER PAINTINGS OF DANCERS HUNG ON THE WALLS OF THE RITZ BALLROOM

Courtesy of Evelyn Escedy

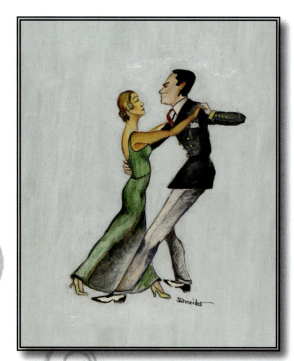

RITZ BALLROOM "AIR CONDITIONING"

Courtesy of Dorothy (French) Vars

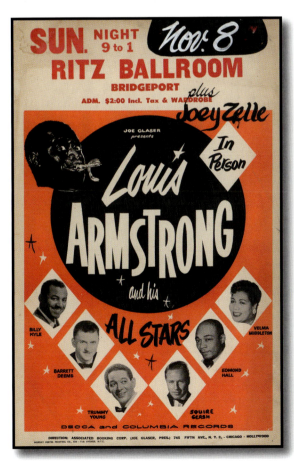
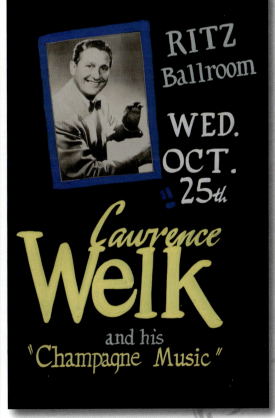

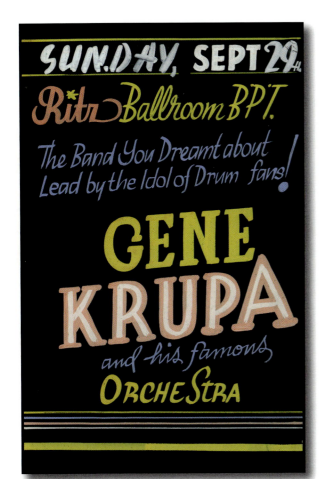

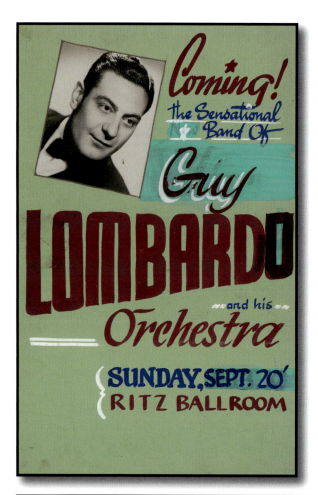
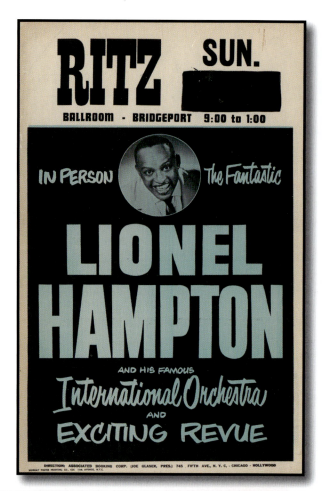

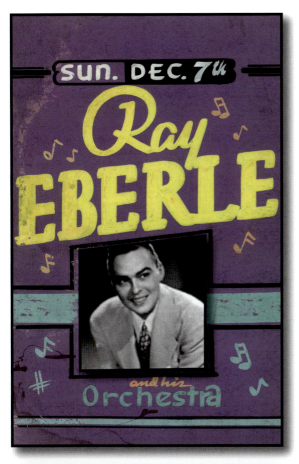

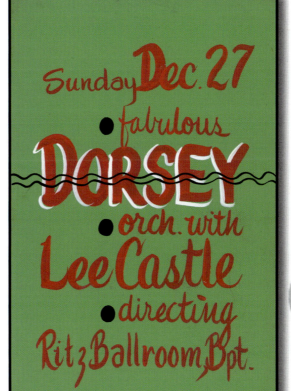

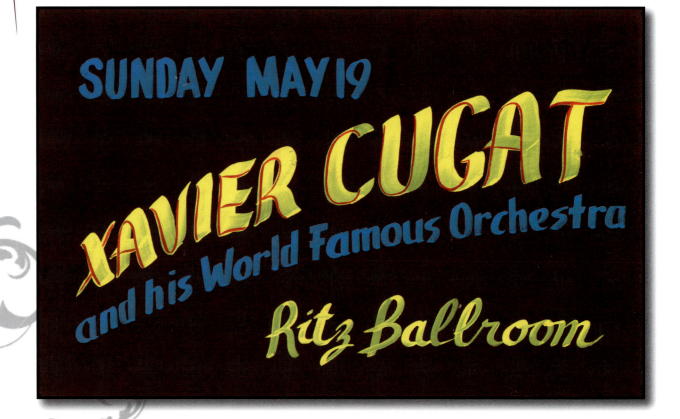

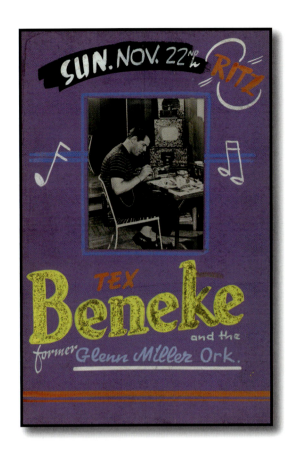
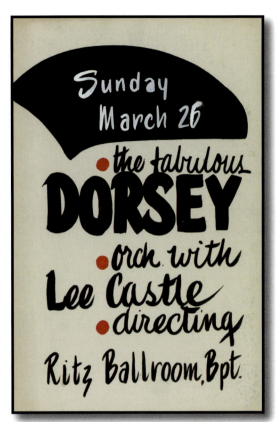
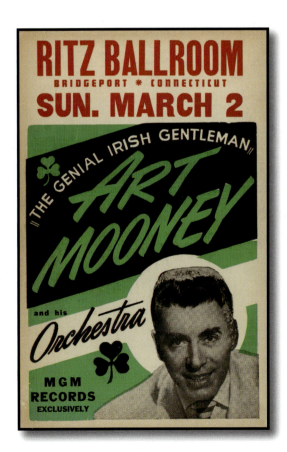
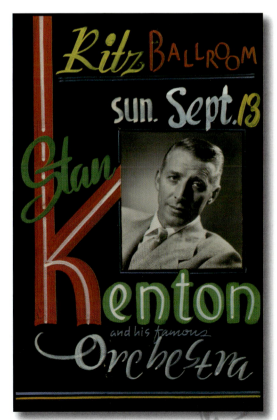

On the bandstand for the last time were Ray Colonari, Joey Zelle, and Joseph Barry.

To the right is Joey Zelle's calendar book page for the last play date at the Ritz. Along with band payments, he indicated the last note he played at the end of the evening . . . A#/Bb. Your author asked him why *that* note and he said,

"It was a melancholy note for a melancholy moment!"

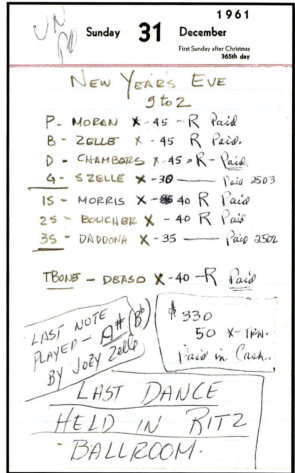

Louis Armstrong

June Christy

Chapter Twelve

Bridgeport Sunday Post, October 22, 1961

The Ritz Passes with Demise of Big Bands: Ballroom Leased to Become Furniture Store

by Roldo Bartimole

Tommy and Jimmy Dorsey

The ballroom dance business, born in the early 1900s, at its peak during the Big Band era of the 1930s, succumbed to the "times" here yesterday with the announced closing of the Ritz Ballroom.

A ten-year lease has been signed with the Breiner Furniture Company, 352 Hancock Avenue, according to Joseph R. Barry, president of Brooklawn Amusement Corp., owner of the Ritz. The dance hall will become a retail furniture outlet, effective February 1, 1962, he said.

"A sad decision," said Mr. Barry, who will be ending a half-century career as owner and manager of the Ritz, which opened in 1910. The Ritz will continue to hold dances, at least through New Year's Eve, an annual dance which is still scheduled. The sale was prompted by economics and family persuasions that the 73-year-old manager "take it easy." Mr. Barry, however, is studying plans to open a theatrical booking agency in Bridgeport.

The changing habits and other interests of its customers were blamed as the causes for the slipping gate receipts by Mr. Barry. Facts and figures are impersonal things. But a business is accountable to their tabulations.

As the crowds dwindled after a period of prosperity in the mid-1940s, banquets, proms, class nights, testimonials and a few wedding receptions were not enough to keep the dance business a paying business. The nostalgia of the Ritz as a memory of high school proms and a meeting place for friends who sometimes became permanent partners, though relics of the past for many Bridgeporters, has little economic consequence in the present.

The impersonal facts and figures became the basis of future memories. The figures are leaning toward the wrong side of the profit and loss ledger. And the memories will have to be born someplace else.

The Ritz had its share of memories starting with the transplanting of the dance floor of the old Brooklawn Pavilion to the Ritz. The floor formed the foundation of a half-century of pleasant keepsakes, enlivened by the music of the great name bands and conversations of countless couples.

Mr. Barry would not attribute the finishing blow to any one circumstance. His reasons are general—changing habits and other interests. For Mr. Barry, a Barnum-like promoter, not opposed to a bit of humbug to enliven an amusement business which has as its purpose to entertain, it ends a path he began unknowingly 52 years ago.

Mr. Barry traced the doomed Ritz back to 1910 when he and the late George S. McCormack created the Brooklawn Pavilion from a turn-of-the-century skating rink. It opened Declaration Day, 1910, with Vincent Lopez and his orchestra. The Ritz was a dream come true to both. Mr. McCormack had been associated with his father in the operation of the old Howard hotel. Mr. Barry had been selling candy and newspaper on railroad trains. The two partners had talked about going into business. Mr. Barry insisted it be the amusement business. When an offer to sell the Brooklawn Pavilion was made to Mr. McCormack, he quickly contacted his future partner. Mr. Barry did not know the Pavilion was a dance hall, but aware it met the qualifications of the amusement business, gave a quick okay. The sale was consummated that afternoon.

The admission price to a dance was 15 cents at the pavilion. It moved to 50 cents at the Ritz. The price of admission to a dance at the Ritz advanced to $2.50.

Specifically, what Mr. Barry has left unsaid, might be summed up with the changing habits of teenagers due to the automobile and the effect television has had on adults.

Mere mention of the Ritz revives memories that go back to pre–World War I days when the automobiles were toys for the well-to-do, when the possibilities of the wireless (radio) were not comprehensible, and when women's skirts still swept the floor.

But the big swing to dancing, ballroom style, made its debut in the 1920s. The female was finding more freedom, the women's vote had been won, Clara Bow was the "it" girl and the Charleston was the rage. (The Charleston, Mr. Barry said, was never allowed at the Ritz because the dance required too much space per couple.)

The Ritz was in full swing with four nights of dancing each week. Familiar downtown conversation ended with a "see you at the dance tonight," Mr. Barry said. Males met females at the dance, they didn't take them, he said. The polka and modern dances were featured on Wednesdays; the square dance and waltz on Thursdays; the Casa Ritz, always a local orchestra, then headed by William Malone, played Saturdays; and Sundays were always reserved for the big name bands. The price was 50 cents and people came from as far as Springfield and the Bronx.

To the teenagers of today the Ritz may be a place to go on Saturday, but then the Ritz *was* Saturday night. Known names were always the feature. All the popular bands of the past five decades played the Ritz. Even Jack Johnson, a former heavyweight-boxing champion, played the viola (the big fiddle) at the Ritz.

One of the early performers who drew large crowds was Texas Guinan, who insisted on being called Miss Guinan in private company. She became famous for her greeting to customers in her own nightclub in New York. "Hello suckers," she saluted the customers and they were gladly "taken in" by her.

Earl Fuller originated the "band leader" style of directing a band, while facing the public, Mr. Barry said. Mr. Fuller never played the Ritz but, Mr. Barry said, he had 20 units working ballrooms and playing at social gatherings. As a trademark, Mr. Fuller had a broken bass drum, symbolizing his motto, "Earl Fuller's music, hard to beat."

Mr. Barry has enriched the Ritz with bits of humbug, most originated by himself. A master mountebank in the affected entertainment business, he has been an integral part of the Ritz's history.

One cold night during a coal shortage his partner told him that they would have to cancel the dance because they were not able to get coal for the furnaces. Mr. Barry, quick to react to disaster, said the show must go on. Instead of producing coal, or a substitute, he brought down two bright red lanterns and placed each on top of an old-fashioned pot-bellied stove. The hint of heat he wished to convey to the crowd worked and the dance proved enjoyable.

Another near disaster was averted when a scheduled appearance of the "Happy Wonder Bakers," a popular group, was cancelled because of a dual booking. The agent promised the group would appear the next week free of charge. Mr. Barry who received the call at 3 p.m. the day of the dance, called a laundry service which provided white coats and bakers' hats. A new band, donned in bakers' uniforms, played.

Later in the evening, Mr. Barry announced the fraud, but quickly warded off the anger of the crowd by passing out free ducats to next week's performance by the "original" bakers.

In 1929, Rudy Vallee sang to 350 customers at the Ritz. Eleven months later, Vallee returned to sing before 3,500 persons. "Life is just a bowl of cherries, don't make it serious," was his theme.

But people were taking life seriously. A depression was forcing somber thoughts. The 20s provided success to the dance hall business, but it exited on a sour note. The depression was offering the first big challenge to the business and the entrepreneurship of Barry and McCormack.

"When people don't have money, the dance business gets hurt, "Mr. Barry said. The crowds thinned as disposable income went for the necessities of life. On his way to the Ritz one morning during the depression, Mr. Barry noticed a billboard sign advertising "Bridgeport Day" followed by a big question mark. A call to the Chamber of Commerce revealed that the Bridgeport businessmen were going to offer a gigantic bargain sale Thursday and buses were going to transport people from surrounding areas into Bridgeport free of charge.

The Ritz management, under Mr. Barry's advice, decided to have a dance for 25 cents. The usual fee was still 50 cents. A lower price had been scorned because, if it was featured, it would attract a crowd detrimental to Ritz's reputation of good conduct at dances.

Some 1,200 came to the dance and the revenue from the concessions and checkroom were excellent. Mr. McCormack, exulted by the success, asked his partner if the merchants were going to have another such night. "Who cares?" said Mr. Barry.

Mr. Barry revealed his plan to have a 25-cent dance each Thursday. They would be called "Prosperity Night," he said. Anything leagued with "prosperity" at that time was successful, he said. So the bargain nights continued until Mr. McCormack approached Mr. Barry and said he thought the dances should be discontinued because the crowd the dances were attracting might lower the Ritz standards. Mr. Barry persuaded his partner to wait until the next dance and observe the crowd and then decide. Mr. McCormack agreed.

The industrious Mr. Barry spent the week asking friends to please come to the dance and be sure to tell Mr. McCormack what a wonderful crowd was at the dance. "Tell him that you are coming back next week with your sewing club," he related. Mr. McCormack, impressed by the offered congratulations on the conduct at the dances, said nothing more about discontinuing the dances. The Thursday night specials carried us through the Depression, Mr. Barry said, with a twinkle in his eyes.

No special announcements were needed when the 1930s blew in with the Big Bands taking over. Ballroom dancing to the name bands was the rage. Benny Goodman was the King of Swing and a new vocabulary developed for those "in the groove." They lined up to see and dance to Goodman, the Dorseys, Artie Shaw, Gene Krupa, Count Basie, Jack Teagarden, and Larry Clinton.

The slow music of the Depression gave way to a free feeling of the 30s. People were ready to burst out and they did—on the dance floor. Through the late 30s and into the 40s the big bands reigned and with them came the development of the name vocalists.

World War II interrupted everything. Males were available to limited quantities and why go to the ballroom to dance with a female friend? But the return of servicemen in 1945 gave a rebirth to the dance halls. It was a short-lived regeneration. With the end of the war also came television, automobiles in greater quantities than ever, and money with places to spend it.

But the rejuvenation was sweet while it lasted.

Vaughn Monroe played before some 3,700 persons in 1945. It was the biggest draw at the Ritz since Rudy Vallee packed 3,300 in 1930. It came near the receipt take that Paul Whiteman and his orchestra established as tops ever at the Ritz years before.

Some 2,700 people came to the Ritz to see Stan Kenton in 1946. Kenton returned two years ago and drew only 750 persons.

Death claimed Mr. McCormack in 1948 and Mr. Barry later bought full ownership of the Ritz with the purchase of his partner's half-share from Mrs. Mary A. McCormack.

The times began taking its toll. Those "other interests" became the major interests and helped thin the crowds. Teenagers became more addicted to rock 'n' roll; the big bands faded; and television became a major source of entertainment. Gone were the simple fox trot, and waltz, and the Debbie, shag, double shag, lindy and jitterbug. The Latin American dances had faded and rock 'n' roll, a descendant of the shag, which was one of the breakaway dances, was supreme among the young.

The disc jockey fed vocals by rock 'n' roll artists to the teenagers and anyone else who listened to the radio. The big band sounds were muted. Disc jockeys also expanded their services and radio stations, schools, churches, civic and private groups began holding "teen hops," attracting potential ballroom customers with a juke box and a disc jockey.

While the teenagers began going to the "hop," the adults were patronizing clubs where liquor was available and music was an added attraction. Even the Ritz began scheduling rock 'n' roll artists. And they were fairly successful, Mr. Barry said. But the changes had doomed the ballroom, according to Mr. Barry, who doesn't believe there is a demand there for dancers of that scale.

The sadness of this "sad decision" will be echoed by many until the memory fades and then is no more.

Ray McKinley

Charlie Barnet

Chapter Thirteen

Bridgeport Sunday Post, December 10, 1961

It's Joe Barry Night Wednesday at Ritz

by Tom Magner

Bridgeport Salutes

America's Greatest Ballroom Impresario

Joe Barry

Wednesday, December 13, 1961

Ritz Ballroom   Bridgeport, Connecticut

Dinner Served at 7:00 Sharp   Dancing - Entertainment

b.y.o.b.   Set-ups provided

$5.00 per person

They'll be playing Joe's song Wednesday night in the Ritz ballroom.

No, not a song written by "Joe" Barry in person, but a song—and maybe more—for Bridgeport's grand guy who, as a one-time vaudeville entertainer, and later years, dance hall proprietor, will be feted at a testimonial dinner by Mr. Barry's many friends in this city.

Come New Year's Day "Joe" will retire as "front" man at the Ritz ballroom on Fairfield Avenue after more than a half-century of presenting the great and near-great dance bands for the entertainment of Bridgeport dance lovers.

The original Ritz orchestra of 1926 will be on hand at the testimonial with the exception of "Billy" Malone, and William Ratzenberger, Sr., tuba player, both dead. Jonas Malone, brother of "Bill," will lead the band of yesterday, accompanied by Mrs. Mary Malone.

A group of dancers has been engaged by the committee on arrangements to depict the Charleston dance of the "Roarin' 20s," and dances made famous during the 30s, 40s, and 50s.

Everything will be "legal" at the event as State Attorney General Albert L. Coles will be the "speaker of the evening." He will be the only speaker. He was selected to speak on the life of "Joe" Barry because of the attorney general's long experience in "show biz" both as a dancer and a musician before taking public office.

Dr. Harold Connolly and Joe Norko will take part in furnishing music for the occasion.

Sheriff William T. Burlant, who was a member of the old Ritz orchestra, is chairman of the tickets committee. Sheriff Burlant and Police Supt. Joseph A. Walsh will make the presentation to the guest of honor. Ray Colonari, of Radio Station WICC, is general chairman of the dinner-dance-tribute to Mr. Barry, and also will act as master of ceremonies.

SHARING MEMORIES OF THE RITZ—Albert L. Coles and Joseph R. Barry share reminiscences during last night's testimonial for Mr. Barry, manager of the Ritz Ballroom, which will close after New Year's Eve after 35 [38] years as a mecca of ballroom dancers. Mr. Coles, state attorney general, played the Ritz both as a musician and dancer years ago. Left to right are Mrs. Barry, Mr. Barry, Mr. Coles and Raymond Colonari, manager of station of WICC, who was master of ceremonies.

Chapter Fourteen

Bridgeport Herald, May 7, 1962

Joseph Barry Killed by Train in Fairfield

SURPRISE FOR BALLROOM OWNER—Joseph R. Barry (left), owner of the Ritz Ballroom, was presented with a cake last night in a surprise ceremony marking 50 years in the ballroom business. Sharing the pleasure are Woody Herman (right), bandleader who was filling an engagement at the Ritz Ballroom, and Dolly Houston, formerly a vocalist with Woody's band. Miss Houston, now retired and a housewife, lives in Trumball. The staff of the Ritz provided the surprise. Ray Colonari was master of ceremonies.

KIN ESTABLISH IDENTITY OF EX-RITZ OWNER
HAD GONE TO RAILROAD STATION FOR TRIP TO NEW YORK CITY
BODY MUTILATED
HE OPERATED BALLROOM 51 YEARS UNTIL IT CLOSED IN 1961

Joseph R. Barry, 73, of 3167 Burr Street, Fairfield, who operated the old Ritz Ballroom 51 [38] years, was struck and killed by a train at the Fairfield railroad station today at 9:15 a.m., Fairfield police reported.

The body was so mutilated that positive identification was at first not available. Later, identification was made by members of the family who were shown the victim's hat, shoes and bridgework found at the scene of the tragedy.

CAR REGISTRATION

An auto registration card in Mr. Barry's name was found on the tracks. Mr. Barry's auto was parked near the spot where the train struck him. In an effort to establish identification, Mr. Barry's son-in-law, Loring Chappel of Weston, was contacted by Fairfield police. Mr. Chappel immediately went to Mr. Barry's home to inform Mr. Barry's wife of the situation.

HEADED FOR THE STATION

Police reported that they learned from the family that Mr. Barry left his home at 8:30 a.m. to take a train to New York City where he planned to see some booking agents. Mr. Barry, it was said, was interested in getting back into the entertainment business.

Except for the engineer and fireman on the train, there were no other witnesses, police said. Sgt. James P. Mastroni and Det. Stephen Zadrovitz who are investigating, said Mr. Barry was struck on the eastbound tracks about 100 feet west of the station platform, by Train 8, the Murray Hill, bound for Boston. It does not stop in Fairfield.

The engineer, Vernon Peterson, halted the train at Round Hill Road, about 850 feet east of the station, and notified police before continuing his trip. Police will question him later about details of the fatality.

SAD DECISION

"A sad decision" was the way Mr. Barry put it when on October 21, 1961, he ended more than a half-century as owner and manager of the Ritz which opened in 1910 [1923].

The dance hall became a retail furniture outlet, when a ten-year lease was signed with the Breiner Furniture Company, 352 Hancock Avenue. At that time, Mr. Barry cited changing habits of former Ritz customers for the slipping gate receipts. The crowds, which once filled the hall to dance to the strains of the big name bands, were not coming anymore.

NEW WAYS

The automobile and television brought new pastimes to Bridgeporters. The nostalgia of the Ritz was a real thing for Mr. Barry who traced the beginnings of the ballroom back to 1910 [1923] when he and the late George S. McCormack had the dance hall built at 3243 Fairfield Avenue. The Ritz was in full swing four nights each week. "Males met females at the dance, they didn't take them," Mr. Barry was known to have said.

NIGHTLY VARIETY

Regulars at the Ritz knew that Wednesday was polka night; Thursday was for square dancing and the Casa Ritz, a local orchestra, played Saturdays. Sunday nights were for the big names.

One of those big names was Rudy Vallee. That was 1929, the Depression had begun, and the Ritz was being challenged financially even then. "When people don't have money, the dance business gets hurt," Mr. Barry had said.

PROSPERITY NIGHT

A real show biz entrepreneur, Mr. Barry even took advantage of the Depression to launch "Prosperity Night" each Thursday at the Ritz. The entrance fee was lowered from 50 cents to 25 cents. The Ritz made it through the Depression, Mr. Barry had commented happily during an interview last October.

The turbulent thirties blew in with ballroom dancing the rage. Customers came from as far away as Springfield and the Bronx to dance to the then-magic names of Goodman, the Dorseys, Artie Shaw, Gene Krupa, Count Basie, Jack Teagarden, and Larry Clinton.

The big bands reigned into the 40s. Then came World War II. But with the return of servicemen came a rebirth of the dance halls. With the end of the war there was more money, automobiles and television—and "other interests," as Mr. Barry had called them.

COULDN'T COMPETE

The Ritz could not compete and Mr. Barry was forced to make the "sad decision." The Bridgeport showman was honored last December at a dinner in the Ritz.

Woody Herman

Tony Pastor at the Ritz

Keely Smith and Louis Prima

Chapter Fifteen

Bridgeport Sunday Herald, May 13, 1962

Music Ends For Joe Barry at a Whistle Stop

PROUD OF HIS GALLERY OF STARS—In his office in the Ritz Ballroom, Joseph R. Barry is constantly reminded of his 50 successful and rewarding years in the dance hall business by his autographed gallery of great band leaders, who appeared at the Ritz. The bandleaders represent over five decades of constantly changing dance music trends.

The remains of Joseph R. Barry, recently retired showman who was struck down and killed by a locomotive at the Fairfield railroad station, were laid to rest Wednesday. It was a tragic end to a long and glamorous career for a great entrepreneur and dean of America's ballroom impresarios. More horrible than the death of his life-long partner, George McCormack, who died of cancer a decade before.

In October of last year, Joe Barry had made the most solemn if not the biggest decision of his long life. He decided to close for all time the portals of his beloved Ritz Ballroom and lease the famous dance emporium for a long term to Mitchell Breiner as a furniture showroom.

And with the last strains of *Auld Lang Syne* New Year's morning, 1962, Barry shut down the Ritz and turned the keys over to Breiner.

JOSEPH R. BARRY'S canny operation of the Ritz through over five decades of prosperity and depression won him the lifelong friendship of many big name-band leaders some of whom (like Rudy Vallee) got their start at the Ritz—and the affection of thousands of grandmothers and grandfathers and their sons, daughters, and grandchildren whose feet danced to romance to engagement to marriage from the Ritz Ballroom.

Joe Barry was 72 when he made his Big Decision six months ago to close down this storied dance hall. It was a difficult one. Up until then he was determined to continue running the Ritz as a ballroom to the end of his life—because he never wanted it said that he stopped the music. But his family counseled him to give up the ballroom and retire.

WHEN THE NEWS of Joe's closing the Ritz broke on Page One, a group of prominent Bridgeporters quickly organized a committee to arrange a big testimonial dinner honoring Barry. And on Dec. 14, Joe was given a rousing send-off at his ballroom by more than 500 of his most devoted friends. Atty. Gen. Albert Coles was the keynote speaker; Ray Colonari of WICC was master of ceremonies—Sheriff William Burlant, Harry Neigher, Police Supt. Joseph Walsh, Capt. of Detectives Dom Conte, William Mulvihill, City Clerk Bill Keller, Leo Redgate, and Joey Zelle spoke; a dozen or more bands of now and yesteryear performed, and the voices of scores of great bandleaders were heard via the magic of tape recording (including those of Vincent Lopez and Rudy Vallee) extolling the sterling qualities of Joe Barry.

JOE BARRY REMEMBERS CHARITIES—When informed that there was $400 extra after the testimonial dinner in his honor, Joe Barry, center, retiring after 39 [38] years as operator of the Ritz Ballroom, informed Ray Colonari, chairman of the dinner, to distribute the money to charity. Accepting in equal shares of the gift are, from left, Sheriff William T. Burlant, in behalf of the March of Dimes; Charles T. Early, Lions Club, for the Connecticut Society for Crippled Children and Adults in support of the club project at Camp Hemlocks; Terrence V. McMahon, for Bridgeport Lodge 36, BPOE, for the Crippled Children's Fund of the State Elks Association in support of the Newington Home for Crippled Children; and Edward A. Dworken.

ALL IN ALL it was one of the greatest testimonial dinners of that year or any year of the 20th century in Bridgeport.

JOE BARRY and George McCormack were mere boys back in 1910 when they conceived the idea of going into show business together. They were members of the A.B.C. Club, a hangout where kids of the East Side of Bridgeport with singing or dancing talent would rehearse and put on minstrel shows. Hundreds of kids paid admission to the Joe Barry Theater in the Barry woodshed.

First teaming up as friends, young McCormack and Barry decided to go into the silent motion picture business, but changed their minds when they found out they hadn't enough change in their pockets.

THEN McCORMACK proposed they buy the Brooklawn Pavilion, which was for sale. George used considerable persuasion and Joe agreed, thinking it was a skating rink they were buying. It wasn't until the night before they opened the Pavilion on Memorial Day of 1910 that Joe Barry discovered he was in the dance business with George McCormack.

FROM THAT DAY in 1910, McCormack and Barry operated the Brooklawn for dances and public soirees—from baby shows to mardi-gras carnivals—and during World War I the place hummed with patriotic endeavors, such as war bond drives and benefit dances. The daring young partners always wore evening clothes as they welcomed their customers, and when the crowds exited, they scrambled out of their tuxedos and into old clothes to clean the place for the next night.

FOR 13 YEARS, from May 30, 1910, to Sept. 2, 1923, Joe and Mac ran the Brooklawn. They worked hard, and they prospered. In 1923, they gave way to progress and the old Brooklawn Dancing Pavilion was no more. The Ritz Ballroom became their new venture, and his late partner, Mac, who bought the finest dance music to the people of Fairfield County for almost two generations . . . Rudy Vallee, Vaughn Monroe, Ozzie and Harriet Nelson, Paul Whiteman, the Dorsey Brotherss, Maynard Ferguson, Mal Hallett, Larry Funk, Claude Hopkins, Isham Jones, Guy Lombardo and his Royal Canadians, to name a few.

LOOKING BACK, Barry recalled is was soon after he and Mac opened the Ritz that they gave Rudy Vallee his first break at the Ritz. It was one night in 1924 that Vallee burned up the Post Road from New Haven to Bridgeport to make his first bid as a crooner at the Ritz Ballroom.

UNDER BARRY and McCormack, the Ritz Ballroom flourished and for years it was rated as the foremost ballroom in New England. Through many decades of watching teenagers and adults doing everything from the Lambeth Walk to the Jitterbug, Joe and Mac endured all types of weather and dance business recessions without permitting the standards and policies of their beloved Ritz Ballroom to be lowered one iota. Keeping their Ritz free of roughhousing paid off handsomely.

BARRY became the partner of Mrs. George McCormack after George's death in 1948, and later bought out her interest in the Ritz Ballroom. Called the "oldest active ballroom impresario in America," Joe wore his crown well. A man of tremendous vitality and with a great capacity for work, Barry could have gone on indefinitely if his family would have let him.

BUT THEY FELT he should retire and enjoy his remaining years. And for four months Joe did enjoy himself, basking in the sun and fishing in Fort Lauderdale, Fla.

He had returned in high spirits from his lengthy vacation last week, and bright and early Monday morning he had driven his car to the Fairfield depot where he was to take a train to New York to have lunch with former show business associates. Joe was mulling over the idea of resuming an avocation of his—scouting and booking talent in other ballrooms and theaters.

He just couldn't remain idle. He had to be doing things.

There were no eyewitnesses to the tragedy that befell Barry as he was waiting for his train to New York at the Fairfield railroad station around 9:15 Monday morning. He was struck down and killed by a rain bound for Boston on the eastbound tracks, about 100 feet west of the station platform.

By some quirk of irony, Barry's brother-in-law, Fred C. Shea, 64, was struck down and killed four years ago at the same spot on those railroad tracks in Fairfield.

Johnny Long

Galli Sisters

Chapter Sixteen

Bridgeport Post, June 12, 1970

Fire Razes Ex-Ritz Ballroom; One-Time Site of 'Big Bands' by Frank W. DeCerbo

Photo by Bridgeport's Corbit Photographic Studios, courtesy of Bridgeport History Center

A Landmark Goes Up In Flames
Blaze Leaves "A Total Loss" in Black Rock
One-Story Building Has Housed Breiner's Furniture Since 1962
Damage Heavy
Loss Runs Into Thousands of Dollars; Several Firemen Hurt

The old Ritz Ballroom, where the Depression generation danced its cares away in the heyday of the big bands in the 1930s and 1940s burned to the ground today. Closed nine years ago as one of New England's most popular dance halls for close to half a century, the building, located at 3243 Fairfield Avenue, in Black Rock, has been housing the Breiner's Furniture store since 1962.

Officials of the furniture firm, headed by Samuel L. Breiner, of 129 Short Hill Lane, Fairfield, were not immediately available for comment today, but acting Fire Chief John F. Gleason described the one-story wooden structure and its contents as "a total loss." Officials said the damage will run into the hundreds of thousands of dollars.

Firefighters were dispatched at 12:24 a.m. after an unidentified person reported a rubbish blaze in the rear of the building. There were three additional calls for help during the fight against the flames. The cause was not determined immediately. Firefighters found the interior of the building ablaze and radioed the Emergency Reporting Service fire control center for additional help.

Assistant Fire Chief Howard Bogey said the structure was "fully involved in flames when I arrived." An investigation has been started by Chief Gleason, the city's fire marshal, to determine the cause.

Chief Gleason said flames spread through the entire interior of the low one-story building, destroying hundreds of pieces of furniture and then mushroomed to the roof. At the height of the blaze, the roof collapsed and flames spread to a basement showroom where additional furniture was stored.

Firefighters were hampered by intense heat and smoke and at one point the two pieces of fire apparatus stationed near the building blistered. Several firefighters received minor burns and cuts. An emergency ambulance was stationed at the scene to give medical aid to firefighters. "There was no way of getting into the building because of the intense flames," Chief Gleason said.

Fire companies from the nearby Black Rock fire station were out of quarters when the fire was reported. They had been assigned earlier at 12:15 a.m. to a fire in the Lorraine Industries plant on Hancock Avenue where sawdust was found ablaze in a factory building.

The first company to arrive was Engine Co. 1 from Middle Street headquarters. Fire personnel radioed for additional help upon arrival after seeing flames inside the building. Assistant Fire Chief John Schmidlin later responded to the scene to aid in directing the firefighters after the Lorraine plant blaze was extinguished.

Firefighters battled the blaze two hours before it was declared under control. Recall was at 2:22 a.m. but firemen were still at the scene at noon today wetting down the smoldering interior of the building. Fire officials said neighbors in the area reported hearing the sound of an alarm bell ringing and an explosion shortly before the fire was reported to the ERS center.

A LANDMARK GOES UP IN FLAMES—Flames are visible in windows as fire swept the interior of Breiner's Furniture company store housed in the former Ritz Ballroom on Fairfield Avenue at an early hour today.

Stan Kenton

Carol Kay

Chapter Seventeen

Bridgeport Post, May 5, 1973

Ritz Had a Colorful History with Proms, Bands, Dinners Opened by McCormack–Barry in 1910 [1923]

Testimonial Dinner at Ritz Ballroom for Sgt. Walter L. Auger, January 24, 1951

The colorful history of the Ritz ballroom with its cavalcade of high school and college proms, name bands, and testimonial dinners, dates back to 1910, when the late Joseph Barry and George McCormack became partners and opened the "Brooklawn Pavilion." Although the partnership began with the small pavilion, it wasn't until it was enlarged and renamed the Ritz Ballroom that their names became synonymous with just about every important event in the 20s, 30s, 40s and 50s that involved the changing moods of the dance business.

Ironically enough, when Mr. McCormack asked Mr. Barry to join him as a partner in the "Brooklawn Pavilion," he thought it was a skating rink. It wasn't until some time later that he found that Mr. Barry, who was raised in East Bridgeport and later became a vaudeville hoofer, had led him into the dance business.

The spectacular blaze today destroyed more than a landmark, it destroyed the birthplace of memories for countless thousands of former high school students who danced on its polished floor and walked its promenades during school proms.

The ballroom remained one of New England's most popular dance halls through the moods of music and dancing of the zany "Roaring 20s," and the more sedate but still frivolous dancing of the 30s. In the 1940s, the partners probably had their more trying years as they attempted to keep the "Lindy Hop" from shaking the Ritz apart as soldiers and sailors home on leaves and furloughs danced to the music of famous bands as Glenn Miller, Tommy Dorsey, Jimmy Dorsey, Harry James, and many others.

The partnership ended in 1948 with the death of Mr. McCormack, but the image of the Ritz survived with Mr. Barry as the owner. Mr. Barry kept pace with the changing times, substituting testimonial dinners in the famous dance hall as interest in dancing to the "big bands" declined rapidly.

It wasn't until 1961 that Mr. Barry succumbed to the changing times, and was forced to admit that television was too formidable an opponent. In what he called one of his "saddest decisions," he signed a ten-year lease with the Breiner Furniture Company, then of 352 Hancock Street.

The colorful saga of the Ritz Ballroom slipped into history on New Year's Eve, 1961, when couples danced there for the last time. Mr. Barry, who had been honored many times for the greatness he had displayed in the operation of the Ritz and the countless charities he had aided, died in 1962 at the age of 73, just a few months after the Ritz ceased to be one of New England's leading ballrooms.

Frosh-Sophs Enjoy Their Spring Prom

On Friday evening, May 5, the Freshman-Sophomore Spring Prom was held at the Ritz Ballroom, Bridgeport, with approximately one hundred and thirty couples dancing to the music of Mal Hallet and his orchestra. From nine to one, the guests danced to a variety of tunes, all of which were played in the same superb manner.

During a short intermission, Connie Sternchak of the Sophomore Class delighted the dancers with a rendition of "My Foolish Heart" and "Bewitched, Bothered and Bewildered."

Refreshments were sold during the entire dance, and coffee and sandwiches were available in the Green Room during the Band's intermission. At that time, the orchestra leader could be seen chatting with some of the guests.

The dance was a colorful affair, the various shades of the dresses mingled with the white jackets, or black tuxedoes providing a study in contrast. At the far end of the ballroom a Fairfield Pennant was hung and it was used as a background for the many pictures which were taken during the evening. Chairman Jack Connell and his committee are to be congratulated for their capable planning and direction of this underclass dance.

Pictured at the Freshman-Sophomore Prom are Chairman John Connell, Miss Jane Aspinwall, Ritz Manager Joseph Barry, and maestro Mal Hallett.

Chapter Eighteen

Bridgeport News, November 1, 2001

Rudy Vallee Once Crooned in Bridgeport
by Mary K. Witkowski

Rudy Vallee, Circa 1929

It was a night to remember in Bridgeport. Rudy Vallee, who had become famous on screen as well as on stage, performed at the Ritz Ballroom. Born in Island Pond, Vermont, his name was originally Hubert Prior Vallee. Rudy attended the University of Maine and later Yale.

It was at Yale that Vallee started his own band, the "Yale Collegians," later called the "Connecticut Yankees." After he graduated from Yale in 1927, Vallee changed his first name to "Rudy" and gained popularity on stage for a style that made him the first to be called a "crooner."

His trademark became a small megaphone, which helped him to be heard over the screams of young women who swooned over his music. Radio helped him spread his popularity, and by 1929, he was in his first movie.

Before coming to Bridgeport to play in March of 1937, Vallee first played for the prom at Yale at his first major engagement at Yale since he left the school in 1927. It was later that evening he arrived in Bridgeport to play at the Ritz.

The Ritz Ballroom was jammed with over a capacity audience, more than 2,500 persons spilling onto the dance floor and surrounding Vallee and his orchestra. A newspaper reporter later said "at the Ritz, he literally floored 'em." The crowd was so great that people in the back couldn't see Vallee and his orchestra. Rudy asked the audience to literally "sit down" right where they were . . . so that people behind them could also enjoy seeing the orchestra. It was the first "sit-down dance" ever staged at the Ritz.

Rudy Vallee continued his popularity on stage and screen, later appearing in guest appearances on television on the *I Love Lucy Show*, and appearing in *Batman* as "Lord Fogg." He died in 1986.

Rudy Vallee and George McCormack, March 7, 1937

Chapter Nineteen

The Ritz by Gene Hull

Claude Thornhill

Bridgeport native and musician Gene Hull in his book Hooked on a Horn *tells the story of a teenager with dreams and aspirations he hoped he would find at the Ritz Ballroom. Here are excerpts from this book's chapter titled, "The Ritz."*

Everyone loved the Ritz. It was the social center, the place for young adults to hear great music and meet each other. My mother said I was too young to go there. "It isn't a place for kids."

By the time I was fourteen and a half, I figured I was old enough. I'd been playing sax for almost three years and thought I knew everything about it. So I proposed that I could learn more quickly by listening to the famous bands live at the Ritz.

"It's an older crowd," she said, "and there's drinking downstairs. Besides, you'd have to take the bus, and you'd be out late. There's school the next day." I explained that was no problem for me. "I don't drink, I'll take the bus. And I'll be home early. Please can I go?"

In the interest of my having a positive learning experience, I believe, she gave in. "All right, but make sure your homework's done first. And be careful. Call me when you get there."

That wasn't quite all there was to it. I had a plan that I didn't tell her about. I was taking my saxophone with me. Most every Sunday night thereafter that's just what I did. The bus that took me to the Ritz was always jammed. Each week I'd board at Park and Fairfield with my sax protected in its pillowcase. I still hadn't gotten a real case for it, but that didn't matter. If my plan worked, I'd soon be able to afford one. I sat up in the front of the bus right behind the driver, cradling the weird-shaped pillowcase, pretending to look out the window at something important. I could tell that other people were looking at me and snickering. I made believe I didn't notice them.

Admission was $1.10 to see the biggest name bands and 75 cents for the not-so-famous ones. Movies were 26 cents in those days, and gas was 15 cents a gallon. The older girl at the ticket booth always said, "Good evening, Gene," giving me my ticket, smiling down at me through the glass, leaning forward so I could hear her through the half-circled hole at the bottom. She had dark hair and a very pretty face. I liked the fact she knew my name, but I wished she wouldn't have been so obvious in greeting me like a little kid with all the adults standing in line. It just attracted attention to my pillowcase and me.

Every time I entered the ballroom the sound of the band's brass section would hit me full in the chest and make my rib cage vibrate. I loved the feeling. The manager kept an eye on me. My mother must have called him. Once inside, my ritual was to walk around the ballroom first, then call my mother to tell her I was fine (the pay phone cost a nickel). Then I'd find a place right next to the bandstand, opposite the entrance, and sit there with my sax on my lap, listening to the music. After staying there for two hours, until intermission, I'd take the 10:05 p.m. bus home.

To me the Ritz was a magical place. I could get next to the world-famous bands and hear their sounds in the closest ring of audience. I liked the jazz-orientated bands best, especially those of Stan Kenton, Boyd Rayburn, Claude Thornhill, Gene Krupa, Charlie Barnett, Benny Goodman, Harry James, and Woody Herman—he was my favorite. Once a month great "colored bands" like Jimmie Lunceford, Count Basie, or Duke Ellington appeared.

The Ritz was a long, white, wood frame building. It had a low ceiling, a sunken dance floor and a capacity of over 3,000 people. That was if people were dancing. But most fans stood, packed in a huge semi-circle in front of the band, absorbing the excitement, limiting the dancing to the extreme ends of the dance floor. One night the crowd actually reached over 4,000 for Guy Lombardo—not my style of band, too "schmaltzy."

From the outside the Ritz didn't look like much. But inside it was elegant with its long, polished hardwood dance floor and glittering chandeliers. Blue and red carpeting covered the elevated promenade that surrounded the sunken dance floor. A white balustered fence with a varnished oak railing on top encompassed much of the dancing area.

Above the floor, accordion-pleated red drapes gathered from the sidewalls, swooping up to the middle of the ceiling and gathered around the chandeliers. The red velvet cushioned benches, which lined the walls, were occupied by dancers or voyeurs who sat between dances and rested, flirted, or just watched the other people.

Downstairs was a noisy bar with a separate soft drink area and a jukebox. I checked it out but never spent much time there. I was at the Ritz to listen and absorb. Besides, everyone there was much older than I, and that was kind of intimidating.

The elevated bandstand was situated along one side in the middle of the ballroom. However, you could walk completely around the ballroom along the promenade, even behind the bandstand, so it was possible to see what music they were playing. Local musicians always gathered behind the bandstand and smoked cigarettes and talked boisterously, like they knew everything, and greeted each other as if they were just as important as the famous musicians up on the bandstand.

I would sit right alongside the bandstand each week, waiting, holding my sax, hoping. This was my plan: someday, it could be tonight, there would be an announcement on the public address system. An important voice would say, "Your attention, ladies and gentlemen. Attention, please. The band's lead alto saxophone player has taken ill. Is there an alto saxophone player in the house?"

I'd be right there. I'd take my sax out of the pillowcase and be ready to play for the famous bandleader who needed me. I'd save the day. I'd be discovered, soon to be famous. This was a real possibility for me. People get sick all the time. So each time I went to the Ritz, I'd say to myself, *Tonight may be the night. I'm ready.* The possibility of the glorious fame of it all gave me more incentive to practice and improve each week.

Faithfully, month after month, I kept the Sunday night vigil. By this time everyone who worked at the Ritz knew me, and people on the bus recognized me. I knew it was just a question of time before the important announcement would come. And I would be up on the bandstand playing my sax with all those wonderful professional musicians.

But no sax player ever took ill, at least not ill enough to stop playing. I listened carefully each Sunday night, but the announcement never came. I even told the manager that

I was "available" and had "my horn with me." "Thank you, Gene," he said. "I'll keep that in mind." He must have been amused.

One wintery Sunday night, about ten years after my "Ritz daze," I was home watching television with my wife and our three young children. The phone rang. It was for me. Ray Colonari, still the manager of the Ritz Ballroom, knew I was a professional musician, since my bands now frequently played in local clubs and for dances and parties at the Ritz. He remembered me from the days when I was a polite little kid going to the Ritz on Sunday nights with my sax and a dream in a pillowcase.

"Gene," Ray said, "How are you? You play sax, right?"

"Sure I do, Ray."

"You play baritone sax, too?"

"Yes I do. Why? What's up?"

"Claude Thornhill's band is playing tonight."

"I know. And it's a fine band. Heard him years ago."

The bells were ringing. Could this be the night? Was it possible? After all these years was I finally getting the call to play with a name band at the Ritz? But on bari sax, not alto? So what. It didn't matter. It was the Ritz, and it was a name band. This was my chance.

"You know Gerry Mulligan, the baritone sax man with the band?"

"Yeah sure. He's famous. One of the best."

"Gerry's horn isn't working right—some key is broken. And I was wondering . . . could we borrow your bari tonight?"

Suddenly I deflated and got depressed. No, that doesn't come close to what I felt. I was crushed. Just when it looked as if the moment might finally be and was dangling right in front of me, poof, it was gone. I suppose it was one of life's little ironies. Everybody gets teased once in a while. It was just my turn. Get over it, I said to myself; you're not a kid anymore, even if you are a dreamer.

"Sure, Ray. I'll bring it right over."

I drove to the Ritz in my eight-year old Plymouth, the bari resting in its case on the back seat. I gave the horn to Ray and never let on how I really felt. I was too proud. I sat alongside the bandstand in my old familiar spot, habit, I guess, and listened to the great Gerry Mulligan play my baritone sax brilliantly. Time flashed back to the many nights, years before, when I was a kid. I remembered the excitement and anticipation and how hopeful I was.

Now as I gazed around the ballroom, I saw that I was older than many of the patrons. Local musicians weren't enclaved behind the bandstand anymore. People no longer gathered en masse in front of the band as in former years, cheering and applauding each individual soloist. They were dancing. The charged atmosphere was gone. The era of big band mass hysteria was in flux, changing to what, I didn't know. But I didn't like it.

After a few tunes, I couldn't listen any more. I got up, found Ray and said, "I'll pick up the horn tomorrow, Ray."

"Fine," he said, "I'll have it right here. And thanks a lot, Gene. You saved the day. I won't forget it."

"Sure. Glad to help. Anytime."

I went outside and moped in front of the Ballroom. I stood there, kind of blurred out. It was snowy and cold. The green and white bus came by and stopped. People got off. I got on. It was brightly lit and almost empty. The floor was wet where snow had been tracked and melted. We bumped and bounced our way back to town. I thought about all the times I went to the Ritz as a kid with my horn. I thought about the music and the fine band I heard that night, and the telephone call, and my family, and playing my sax, and never playing in a name band . . . or even being a movie star.

Twenty minutes later I got off at my stop and walked home. The next morning I went outside to get in my car. It wasn't there. I shook my head, a little puzzled. Then I remembered it was still parked out at the Ritz. So was my saxophone.

Gene Hull at the Ritz

Madeline Russell

Larry Clinton

Chapter Twenty

Memories Are Made of This

VAUGHN AND US . . . *Vaughn Monroe, the "man with the band" was "tops" at the Ritz Ballroom last Sunday evening. Vaughn first began to toot a trumpet in Akron, Ohio, and won a state-wide trumpet contest while at the tender age of 15. He originally set his sights on an operatic career enrolling at Carnegie Tech and majoring in voice. His interests, outside the music field, are headed by a proud, beaming father-like recitation of the doings of his two daughters, Candy and Christine, aged two and five. Then, of course, our favorite is an airplane pilot and a top-notch motorcycle driver. He is definitely a southpaw, using his left hand to autograph and propel a baton. One of his hobbies is photography and the famed bandleader deserves an assist on the pic on this page as he checked and rechecked the various functions which had to be performed by shutter lady, Lillian Shepard, before she recorded on film the visit of the Youth Reporters. After answering a barrage of questions, Vaughn Monroe took time out to pose for a pic with the Youth Page reporters.*

In left to right order are: Sarah Vena, Pearl Toth, Ray Ziko, Rosemary Mercurio, and Vaughn.

Perhaps the most touching memories of the Ritz Ballroom are the personal remembrances of the thousands who were regular patrons. Here we present various memories shared by regional residents as well as those famous music makers who visited the Ritz or who were featured on the bandstand.

Peggy (Middlemass) Steucek of Bridgeport seems to be the unofficial Ritz historian of the area, who describes the Ritz as being, "The size of half a football field." She actually worked for Joe Barry from 1957 until the Ritz closing as a sign painter. Her job was to paint the various placards that were placed around the community, many of which are featured in a colorful section of this book. Her "sign room" was downstairs at the Ritz, next to the band room where they changed and stored their gear. Her first sign job was for an upcoming appearance by Xavier Cugat. After painting twenty signs using the letter "Z" for his first name, she discovered her error and had to laboriously redo her work. Peggy fondly remembers the time that Louis Armstrong visited her sign room and sat and chatted with her for a while. She recalls how warm and regular a person Armstrong was, like an old friend.

Louis Armstrong autographed a picture for Peggy (Middlemass) Steucek

Another of Peggy's Ritz memories include being asked by Ritz Manager Ray Colonari to go onstage and pin a corsage on Armstrong's vocalist, Vilma Middleton, enjoying performances by the Policeman's Pipe Band and, of course, dancing with her husband-to-be, Peter Steucek. Along with meeting all the famous bandleaders and singers, Peggy feels her fondest memory of the Ritz was bringing Joe Barry his weekly signs and sitting with him as he regaled her with his many stories of the Ritz's earliest days.

Peggy Middlemass and future husband Peter Steucek

Wedding receptions were popular at the Ritz as interest in the big bands waned. Among the many happy couples who had their receptions at the Ritz were **Rita and Robert Mencel, Thomas Katsis, Joan and Edward Gawitt, Frances and Andrew Cretella** and former Stratford Superintendent of Schools **John Olha and his wife, Mary.**

Andrew Paul enjoyed going to the Ritz in the mid-forties. He recalls the soda fountain and enjoying the delicious ice cream sundaes for a quarter while listening to the great bandleaders. He also remembers Pat Grant, the longtime policeman at the Ritz entrance. Paul also remembers meeting almost every bandleader and vocalist who appeared at the Ritz and getting autographed photos (seen throughout this volume).

Cretella wedding with Joe Barry in background

Rosemary and Howard Williams remember first meeting at the Ritz and the fun they shared at numerous Ritz dates and dances thereafter. Rosemary recalls seeing a very young, skinny, bow-tied and relatively unknown Frank Sinatra performing with the Harry James Orchestra. A big thrill for her occurred in December of 1946 when, as co-editor of Stratford High School's *Clarion* newspaper, she was one of several teens to meet and interview Vaughn Monroe.

Gawitt Wedding

Harry James at the Ritz

Rosemary Mercurio's souvenir photo from Sinatra performance at the Ritz.

Artie Shaw at the Ritz

Tom Katsis loved dancing at the Ritz in the late forties. He remembers Gene Krupa commenting that he loved playing at the Ritz. Other bandleaders he enjoyed were Joey Zelle, Jack Still as well as vocalist Manning Cox. Tom comments, "I spent the greatest day of my life—my wedding day—at the Ritz!"

Carol Costello, niece of Ritz co-founder George McCormack, remembers that management was strict about dancers dancing "too close." Her uncle was quite the dancer, and left the business end of management to partner Joe Barry.

Acclaimed bandleader **Artie Shaw** was raised in New Haven, Connecticut. In an interview on *The Ritz Ballroom Hour*, Shaw remembered visiting the Ritz Ballroom in 1927 to see the Gene Goldkette Band. It would be only a dozen years later that Shaw catapulted to big band fame with such hits as "Begin the Beguine," "Stardust," "Frenesi," and "Moonglow," and was a regular performer at the Ritz leading his own orchestra.

Ken Stumbers remembers a newsboy Christmas Party at the Ritz in the late 1950s.

Kathy (Sadler) Lasky's earliest recollection of the Ritz Ballroom was playing dress-up with her girlfriend in gowns their mothers wore at the Ritz. As a child she attended many weddings and showers and company Christmas parties at the Ritz. As one of only two female newspaper carriers back in the 1950s, Kathy enjoyed the paper's incentives to get new customers . . . a free dinner at the Christmas banquet held at the Ritz. She remembers going there with the other girl carrier and seeing a whole sea of boys. In later years she lived in Black Rock, and remembers tearfully the fire and the subsequent tearing down of the historic building. She tells her children and grandchildren about her Ritz memories, especially about when her dad forced her to dance with her brother after having to stand on her dad's feet and learn the steps of the Waltz. Her dad wanted his children to be good dancers, and it worked!

Ed and Ann Mastrone enjoyed dancing to Vaughn Monroe, Carmen Cavallero, and Gene Krupa at the Ritz.

Vaughn Monroe once commented about his performances at the Ritz, "I only wish we received such a warm response from all the audiences we entertain as the one we receive here in Bridgeport which is sort of a boom town for us."

Terry Burns was at the Ritz one evening when the pay phone on the wall was ringing and no one bothered to answer it. After a number of rings, she decided to pick up the phone. The voice on the other end asked to speak with Louis Prima, who was performing on the Ritz stage at that moment. When Terry informed the calling party about the situation, she was asked to please inform Prima that Keely Smith, Prima's wife, just had the baby!

Ernest Ferrari enjoyed visiting the Ritz, Lyric, Globe, and Pleasure Beach Ballrooms to hear Benny Goodman, the Dorseys, Earl Hines, Glen Gray and the Casa Loma Orchestra, among other bands.

Flo Amalfitano was a vocalist with Ronny Rommel's band at the young age of sixteen. She sang under the stage name "June Haven" and has warm memories of entertaining the many Ritz dancers.

Helen Shaw, the "little girl with the big voice," and **Manning Cox** were longtime vocalists with Joey Zelle's band.

Sal DePiano recalls what a thrill it was to get into the Ritz. Often while listening outside with his friends with no money for the admission, Sal remembers McCormack and Barry, both very unassuming gentlemen, coming outside and letting them in for free. He describes the Ritz as a warm, active and enjoyable setting where everyone from Barry, McCormack, and even policeman Pat Grant at the door seemed to fit together. There was never a problem, no fights . . . people were genuinely there for a good time and not trouble. Sal's memories also include the colorful ceiling bunting and sunken dance floor and how much he enjoyed dancing with his wife who was a good dancer. A musician himself, he remembers playing bass on the bandstand at the Ritz. In the fifties Sal was proud to represent Joe Barry as his attorney, but remembers quite a "different" Joe Barry in early 1962, obviously having taken it very hard after the Ritz closed.

Isabelle Tedesco Garamella was another popular vocalist at the Ritz. She began going to dances when she was sixteen in 1938 with her brother Dominic as chaperone. She always saved the last dance for him. Isabelle always said how wonderful George McCormack was to her, always having a fresh gardenia corsage waiting for her. One of the bands she sang with at the Ritz was the Vinnie Wilson Orchestra. She also was thrilled to meet "the handsomest fella that she ever met"—Victor Mature—at Bridgeport's 3rd War Loan Drive.

Louis Prima is treated to some pizza during Ritz appearance break by local vocalist Isabelle (left) and Prima's beautiful prima dona vocalist, Lily Ann Carol

Ronny Rommel Band with vocalists June Haven and Joe Polseno

Vocalist June Haven

Vocalist Isabelle with Vinnie Wilson Orchestra

Local vocalist Isabelle with actor Victor Mature

Frankie Carle and daughter, vocalist Marjorie Hughes

Frankie Laine

Frankie Carle, piano playing bandleader, was popular with local audiences when he appeared at the Ritz. In a conversation on *The Ritz Ballroom Hour*, Carle remembered playing there one evening with the Mal Hallett Band when a young dancer came up to the bandstand asking to sing a song. "What would you like to sing?" asked Carle. "I'd like to sing "Shine," he replied. Hallett agreed and the song was sung. Afterward the young aspiring singer asked for $25 bus fare to return to home in Chicago. Carle happily accommodated the young man, and all was well.

It seems that this young Sicilian singer was a devoted dance-marathon participant, who traveled throughout the East Coast to all the major dance halls to earn money during the Depression days. On another visit to Bridgeport, he was invited to stay overnight by his local Sicilian friends. He ended up staying at the home of Mary and John Mercurio, this author's grandparents, who told me this story many years ago.

By the way, the name of this Sicilian dancer and aspiring singer from Chicago was Frank LoVecchio. In 1946, when he recorded the song "That's My Desire," which became his first of twenty-three gold records, he changed his name to **Frankie Laine**. Visiting him in his San Diego hilltop home in 1999 was thrilling for your author, especially when he remembered my grandparents and spoke so fondly about his visits to Bridgeport and the Ritz Ballroom. A footnote to this story is that Laine and his partner still hold the record for the longest number of hours on the floor in dance marathon history.

Donald MacAdams recalls that when he was a child his dad was doing business with Columbia Records. In 1938, the advertising manager took thirteen-year-old MacAdams and his dad over to the Ritz and both were introduced to Gene Krupa. It was especially thrilling to young MacAdams as he was a beginning drummer at the time.

Kaye Williams, founder of Bridgeport's Captain's Cove Seaport, enjoyed working as a young teen at the Ritz for his uncle George McCormack, much to his mother's dismay.

Rosemary Tozzi had many fun times and pleasant memories of the Ritz. She and her friends would take two buses to get there to listen and dance to the big bands, Joey Zelle, and the Wednesday night polkas.

Walter Gregory, an "old Black Rocker," spent many evenings at the Ritz.

Sarah Vena Masso enjoyed C.Y.O. dances at the Ritz and remembers also seeing Lawrence Welk (along with the champagne glass and bubbles) and how she and her friends made fun of the band (only to be a faithful TV watcher of Welk years later). She comments it was such a wonderful place for those her age as they were growing up. The Ritz had a dress code that included jackets, tie, shirt—no dungarees or sneakers. No alcohol was sold there and if you had it on your breath they would put you out. She never recalls any fights or violence at the Ritz. When she and her friends were permitted by their parents to go to the Ritz they felt that they had reached "adulthood." The girls always dressed in their finest clothes. In later years, at class reunions, everyone always talks about the good times at the Ritz.

Frank Yankovic, "America's Polka King"

This following narrative was contributed by Sarah and is printed with her permission. It echoes similar moments and memories of the many couples who first met at the Ritz and became life partners.

On December 15, 1951, the fabulous Ritz Ballroom in Bridgeport was the setting of a romantic beginning of our courtship, with its revolving overhead crystal mirror-light balls, and the dim lighting on the dance floor.

This was my first date with Frank Masso. He was recently discharged from the U.S. Marines after serving six years, and had just returned from Korea. We stood by the railings that surrounded the dance area, and watched the dancers finish a number. I had wanted to look special, so I had made a black crepe and velvet dress for this date. Frank wore his powder blue zoot suit with peg pants, a silk embroidered dragon tie from Korea, blue and yellow suspenders, and of course, his blue suede shoes. He was so strikingly handsome.

I believe that the band was the Joey Zelle Orchestra. They started another tune, and Frank asked me to dance. As we walked down a few steps onto the ballroom's polished hardwood floor, the song "Where or When" was playing. Frank put his strong arms around me as we danced this number, and somehow I felt very comfortable with him. We did not say a word to each other, but listened to the words of this song. Somehow it made me feel that I had known Frank for a long time, as this song touched our hearts. Some of the words in this song were: 'We looked at each other in the same way then but I can't remember where or when. For some things that happened for the first time seem to be happening again. And as I feel you so close to me, we smiled before, we laughed before, we loved before, but who knows where or when.'

This song seemed to confirm our feelings for each other. That following week, Frank asked me to go steady. Then on February 14, 1952, he proposed to me. On April 19, 1952, we were married in Blessed Sacrament Church with

Two happy Ritz dancers

a beautiful wedding day. I was wearing a wedding gown that I made. I knew Frank only four months and nine days till the day that we were married. The song "Where or When" has a special meaning to us—Yes, it still can captivate my heart whenever I hear the song playing for it brings back the beginning of our life together, our first date as we fell in love at the Ritz Ballroom, and all the countless blessings that God has given to us.

Note: Frank Masso died on July 23, 2011.

Ed Masaitis recalls growing up in back of the Ritz. "During the 50's, the Ritz Ballroom played an important part in our family's life. The Ritz not only existed in our back yard, 28 Montgomery Street- Black Rock, it provided us our entertainment and part of our livelihood. I was a young impressionable boy when my mother took a job as grill manager and hostess in that wonderful ballroom. Being someone who appreciated what this venue could provide for the family, Ceil Masaitis, my mother, became fast friends with Joe Barry, but also with all of the many wonderful entertainers that came through town to play the Ritz. My sister, Ceil Masaitis (14) and I would often find the entertainers in our kitchen. People like The Crew Cuts, Guy Lombardo, and Vaughn Monroe with my mother who was feeding them before their show. The Crew Cuts sang and warmed up in our kitchen.

1950's Ritz dancing with Joe Barry watching over to ensure all had a great time.

Every night that there was a performance, I could be found somewhere in the Ritz Ballroom, gaining an appreciation for the music of that era. On my tenth birthday, Vaughn Monroe called me up on the stage saying it's little Eddie Masaitis' tenth birthday, and he led everyone in singing Happy Birthday. Another time Joe Barry, sympathizing with us for the loss of our dog, gave us a new Irish Setter puppy and named her Ritzy. At Christmas there was a show for the children with Santa passing out gifts.

Almost all of the performers were happy to sign promotional pictures for my mother. We moved from Black Rock to Miami in 1957, leaving the Ritz Ballroom behind, but the memories went with us and we often repeated the stories to our extended family. Somehow, it made us feel important as if we were part of a very special time and place. Looking back, I think we actually were.

Everyone who visited the Ritz Ballroom made their own personal memories. The last few pages of this book are devoted to readers' own journal entries and memorabilia. In this way, "Home of Happy Dancers" will become a very personal and meaningful family keepsake for future generations.

Artie Shaw

Bea Wain

Epilogue

In this world most everything must end. How we adjust to life's many endings, in the final analysis, determines the course of the rest of our lives.

When over five decades of a life are devoted to fun and merriment, initially as a partnership and then presided over as a sole individual, the line between the person and the project becomes blurry . . . they seem to blend into one thing. Such is the situation that befell Joseph Barry after the lease was signed. There were no more crowds eager to visit, no more touring big bands and orchestras to book, no more memories to be made. The music had stopped . . . and the magic had ended.

For Joe Barry the memories were not enough to sustain him, not enough to relish and remember in his remaining years. With nothing to look forward to tomorrow, the decision was made by him to not have any more tomorrows. Thus Barry, the impresario who brought good times, music and fun to so many for so long, ended his life in a most tragic way just months after the Ritz ended.

As mentioned at this book's start, with Barry gone, and his family not realizing it, the Ritz Ballroom office was never cleared out. The photographs, documents, posters, records and memorabilia from over fifty years were the last traces of the glory days and stood silent on the walls and shelves and in the desks that became the partners' second home.

It was to be the fire in April 1970 that brought the final ending of the Ritz. In the old office, on the shelves, on the walls and in the managers' desks and files, all the treasured reminders perished. The blaze drew people from near and far to witness the end of an era, for some the end of their youth, and the end of simpler times, as the big white building fell . . . so many endings.

With the most wonderful documents and artifacts gone, it was your author's mission to recover what might have still existed in the attics and scrapbooks of those who value such keepsakes. Many found their way into this book for us all to enjoy. Should there be more artifacts still in existence, your author encourages their owners to contribute them to the Bridgeport History Center at the Bridgeport Public Library for safe keeping and preservation for future generations to enjoy.

The Ritz Ballroom will forever live in the memories and hearts of those who remember, symbolic of thousands of other such dance palaces that once dotted America. It is this author's hope that readers of this volume will have gained a sense of respect and renewed appreciation for all such historic venues and will work towards preserving those remaining places rather than witness their slow disappearances across the land.

About the Author

JEFFREY C. WILLIAMS has been an admirer of the Ritz Ballroom since first hearing about it from his parents. A lover of big band music and the Great American Songbook, he often feels he was born too late, as he would have loved to enjoy the music of the 30's and 40's firsthand. In 1997, Jeff began broadcasting a weekly radio show called The Ritz Ballroom Hour on WICC 600AM out of Bridgeport, Connecticut. This powerful station, only three years younger than the Ritz itself, provided Jeff the opportunity to share the music he loves in Sunday night broadcasts to listeners throughout the region. Choosing Sunday nights for his show was no accident as it was Sunday evenings that the name big bands played at the Ritz. Initially, the show covered the music during the decades of the Ritz Ballroom, from 1923 to 1961. His loyal listeners helped him earn a rating of "most listened to" in his time slot. Two years into the show, he moved it to the non-commercial Fairfield University station, WVOF 88.5 FM, and gave it a new name. Now in its fifteenth year of broadcasting, *At The Ritz!* blends vintage music from the big band era with old and new recordings of tunes from the Great American Songbook. His numerous regional stage shows, dances, concerts and dinner theatre productions have been labors of love as he provided entertaining live music options for residents of Fairfield County. In addition, Jeff has been involved in several modern-day Ritz projects. In his position as Program Manager at Bridgeport's Klein Memorial Auditorium back in the mid 1990s, Jeff helped stage a concert featuring the Tommy Dorsey Orchestra. He persuaded his bosses to include a colorful life-size rendering of the interior of the Ritz as a backdrop. During the first tune led by bandleader Buddy Morrow, Jeff pulled back the black drapery, revealing the breathtaking visual along with two couples swing dancing on either side of the band. People were blown away! Another thrilling Ritz moment a few years later 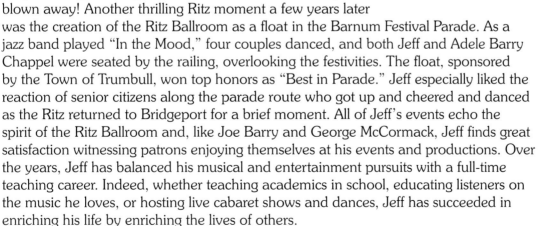 was the creation of the Ritz Ballroom as a float in the Barnum Festival Parade. As a jazz band played "In the Mood," four couples danced, and both Jeff and Adele Barry Chappel were seated by the railing, overlooking the festivities. The float, sponsored by the Town of Trumbull, won top honors as "Best in Parade." Jeff especially liked the reaction of senior citizens along the parade route who got up and cheered and danced as the Ritz returned to Bridgeport for a brief moment. All of Jeff's events echo the spirit of the Ritz Ballroom and, like Joe Barry and George McCormack, Jeff finds great satisfaction witnessing patrons enjoying themselves at his events and productions. Over the years, Jeff has balanced his musical and entertainment pursuits with a full-time teaching career. Indeed, whether teaching academics in school, educating listeners on the music he loves, or hosting live cabaret shows and dances, Jeff has succeeded in enriching his life by enriching the lives of others.

To learn more about Ritz projects and events visit

www.attheritz.org

Resources and Acknowledgements

This book would not have been possible without
the invaluable assistance of the following:

BRIDGEPORT HISTORY CENTER
at the Bridgeport Public Library
Mary K. Witkowski, Director

*Assorted Editors, Writers, and Photographers
of the former*
BRIDGEPORT POST & TELEGRAM
and former
BRIDGEPORT HERALD

*Very special thanks are extended to the following
for their significant contributions to this book:*

*LES BROWN
LES BROWN, JR.
FRANKIE CARLE
ADELE BARRY CHAPPEL
EVELYN ESCEDY
FRANKIE LAINE
EDWARD MASAITIS
ARTIE SHAW
DON SIGOVICH
PEGGY STEUCEK
JOEY and MARIAN ZELLE*

JACK BEHRENS, *Author*
Big Bands & Great Ballrooms: America is Dancing . . . Again
AuthorHouse/2006

RICHARD GRUDENS, *Author*
Star Dust: The Bible of the Big Bands
Celebrity Profiles Publishing/2008

GENE HULL, *Author*
Hooked on a Horn: Memoirs of a Recovered Musician
Trafford Publishing/2005

Acknowledgments and thanks are also offered to the dozens of area residents
for sharing their Ritz remembrances, artifacts and vintage photos
that collectively add authenticity and perspective to this project.

Happy Memories

Use these pages to make journal entries, write personal rememberances or affix your own photos, memorabilia and mementos of the Ritz!

The Ritz

NEXT SUNDAY EVENING — NOV. 26th

BROOKLAWN DANCING PAVILION 1910-1922  RITZ BALLROOM 1923-1961

By Special Request & Popular Demand

Featuring
1 Step, Waltz
& 2 Step

GRAND RE-UNION
And
OLD TIMERS' NIGHT

Presenting
Fox Trot
Modern &
Latin Tunes

JOEY ZELLE and the Casa Ritz Orchestra
12 MUSICIANS & VOCALIST. Distinctive - Delightful - Danceable.
This has been the House Band of the Ritz for the past 14 years.
8:30 P.M. TO 12:30 A.M.   ADMISSION INC. W/ROBE $1.00

A Nite Long to be Remembered

| Next Record Hop Wed. Eve. Nov. 22 Thanksgiving Eve | COME ONE — COME ALL NO DANCE TONIGHT Your Host, Joseph R. Barry | Rhythm & Blues Sil Austin & the Chantels Thanksgiving Nite Thurs., Nov. 23 |

Tonight  **CONTINUOUS DANCING**

THE WAR IS OVER — BUT THE MUSICAL BATTLE OF NOTES IS ON — THE SPARKS ARE FLYING! PLENTY OF "HIT" AND "BELOW THE BELT" TUNES.

2 BANDS 2
22 — MUSICIANS AND ENTERTAINERS — 22
JAM SESSION FEATURING TOP FLIGHT ARTISTS OF EACH BAND
PRESENTING
RONNY ROMMEL, formerly of Louis Prima's Band, and the Casa Ritz Orchestra of 1947 and
JOEY ZELLE, formerly of Ronney Rommel's Band, and the Current Casa Ritz Orchestra

Soloists
Helen Shaw   Manning Cox
Joe Polseno   Dolly Houston
$1.00 Adm. Incl. Tax & Wrobe, $1.00

TUESDAY, Feb. 10th—Pre-Lenten Polka Time Dance with Polonia Radio Orchestra of Hartford.
FRIDAY—Sea Scouts Bridge Of Honor.
SATURDAY—Joey Zelle and the Casa Ritz Orchestra.
SUNDAY, Feb. 15—Buddy Rich | SUNDAY, Feb. 22—Frankie Carle

RITZ BALLROOM

For Your Pleasure DANCE  New England's Most Beautiful BALLROOM

TONIGHT—FRIDAY
ANNUAL BASSICK-FAIRFIELD FOOTBALL HOP
Next Square Set Party With Irv Hintz and Tommy — Nov. 26
TOMORROW IS SATURDAY—MAKE YOUR DATE NOW
JOEY ZELLE AND CASA RITZ ORCHESTRA

SWEET   **SUNDAY**   STYLIZED
BLUE BARRON
AND HIS M.G.M. RECORDING ORCHESTRA
"MUSIC OF YESTERDAY AND TODAY"

| WED., THANKSGIVING EVE. FRANK WOJNAROWSKI Door Prizes — Turkeys — Candy | THANKSGIVING NITE **JERRY WALD** |

RITZ BALLROOM, Bridgeport

JOHNNY LONG

Johnny Long, the only southpaw violinist who is famous, brings his orchestra to the Ritz bandstand on Sunday evening, May 11. Straight from the campus of Duke University the band has become the all-time favorite band with students everywhere, which has earned them the name of "Young America's Favorite."

Every Saturday night come and dance to "music as you like it" featuring Joey Zelle and the ever popular Casa Ritz orchestra.

On Sunday night, May 18, the Ritz presents Ray McKinley and his orchestra for your dancing pleasure.

Sunday, Jan. 23rd
THOSE FABULOUS DORSEYS
TOMMY DORSEY
and his Orchestra
featuring
JIMMY DORSEY
with
BUDDY RICH — LEE CASTLE
LYNN ROBERTS — BILL RAYMOND
Direct from the
Jackie Gleason TV Show

Every Saturday Nite
JOEY ZELLE'S
Casa Ritz Orchestra
Presenting Pyramid Record's
BUZZ CRAIG

Sunday, January 30th
Swing and Sway with
SAMMY KAYE
and his Orchestra

Happy New Year To All — McCormack & Barry

Tonite RITZ BALLROOM BPT. DANCE DATES YOU CAN'T AFFORD TO MISS!

"AMERICA'S YOUNG SINGING FAVORITE"
RAY EBERLE
AND HIS ORCHESTRA
WITH ROSEMARY CALVIN — BILLY MAXTED
ADMISSION INCL. TAX AND WROBE, $1.80

CELEBRATE **New Year's Eve** HERE
DANCING 9:00 P.M. TO 2:00 A.M.
JOEY ZELLE
AND THE CASA RITZ ORCHESTRA
Featuring ● Helen Shaw — Soloists ● Manning Cox

★ GRAND MARDI GRAS ★ GALA CARNIVAL ★
SOUVENIRS, FAVORS & HATS FREE TO ALL WHO ATTEND!
DRESS OPTIONAL — NO RESERVATIONS NEEDED
$1.80 — ADM. INCL. TAX & WROBE, $1.80

| Tuesday Evening Tri-Y Club Christmas Hop | No Dance New Year's Night January 1st. |
| Tomorrow Night Bassick/High Christmas Formal. | Friday Night — January 2nd, Irving Hintz, Tommy & The Farmers |

Sunday, Jan. 4th — AL GENTILE - And His New Englanders

SUNDAY
Young America's Favorite
JOHNNY LONG
and His Orchestra

EVERY SATURDAY
JOEY ZELLE
and the
Casa Ritz Orchestra

Sunday, May 18th
RAY McKINLEY
and his Orchestra

RITZ BALLROOM
BRIDGEPORT, CONNECTICUT
NEW ENGLAND'S HOME OF NAME BANDS

SUNDAY, MARCH 5
It's the Band They're All Talking About
AL LOMBARDY His Clarinet and Orchestra
and including THE DIXIELAND FIVE

| EVERY SATURDAY JOEY ZELLE and The Casa Ritz Orchestra | EVERY WEDNESDAY Polish and Modern Dancing |

SUNDAY, MARCH 12
The Genial Irish Gentleman
ART MOONEY

FRIDAY, MARCH 17
ST. PATRICK'S NITE
Mardis Gras and Dance
2 BANDS 2
Club Ritz Orchestra Plus
Irv Hintz—Tommy & Farmers

FLASH — COMING SUNDAY, MAY 7 — **FLASH**
RALPH FLANAGAN and His Sensational Orchestra

It Is Always a pleasure to Serve the
UNIVERSITY OF BRIDGEPORT AT THE RITZ BALLROOM

TUESDAY
FLASH! FLASH!
First of a Series of
JAM SESSIONS & DANCE
"NATE" SUSSMAN
AND HIS CATS AND JAMMERS

PETE MONSY	JOE ZELLE	REX VALERO
ED GRAF	STEVE HUDAK	HORACE SILVERS
HOWIE MARKS	ERNIE CHRISTOPHER	LARRY MARKS
	JOE WATKINS	

8:00 to 12:00 — Four Hour Session. Adm. incl. tax & wrobe. 75c
COME ONE—COME ALL—YOU'LL ENJOY EVERY SECOND OF IT!

Tonight

TOMORROW NIGHT
"THE YOUNG

AND
Featuring
AD

VA
AND HIS
The Moonm

THURSDAY, N
TONITE — Stu